Out of the Dust

Out of the Dust: Stories of Hope from Mozambique

Copyright © 2025 Steven Lazar

All rights reserved. No part of this publication may be reproduced in a retrieval system, or transmitted in any form or by any means—electronic, mechanical, photocopying, recording, or otherwise—without the prior written permission of the publisher.

Scripture passages have been taken from the Holy Bible, New International Version, NIV Copyright 1973, 1978, 2011 by Biblica, Inc. Used by permission. All rights reserved worldwide.

This manuscript has undergone viable editorial work and proofreading, yet human limitations may have resulted in minor grammatical or syntax-related errors remaining in the finished book. The understanding of the reader is requested in these cases. While precaution has been taken in the preparation of this book, the publisher and author assume no responsibility for errors or omissions, or for damages resulting from the use of the information contained herein.

This book is set in the typeface *Athelas* designed by Veronika Burian and Jose Scaglione.

Paperback ISBN: 978-1-923067-19-6

A Publication of *Tall Pine Books*
PO Box42 | Warsaw, Indiana 46581
www.tallpinebooks.com

| 1 25 25 20 16 02 |

Published in the United States of America

Out of the Dust

Stories of Hope from Mozambique

Steven Lazar

"From the moment I encountered Steve and Ros Lazar in 2001 at our Iris Centre in Zimpeto, I knew they were catalysts for transformation. Their unwavering passion and dedication to uplifting the community were nothing short of inspirational.

In "Out of the Dust," we see a tapestry of hope, resilience, and love. This book is a beautiful testament to the power of compassion and the extraordinary changes that can arise from even the most challenging circumstances. With each page, we are invited to witness transformed lives, reminding us that even in the face of adversity, there is always a path to renewal.

"Out of the Dust" is not just a story. It's a celebration of the human spirit and the joy that can emerge from the ashes of hardship. I wholeheartedly recommend this uplifting read to anyone seeking inspiration and a deeper understanding of the remarkable potential for change that lies within us all. Get ready to be moved, inspired, and filled with hope!

Steve and Ros Lazar have made a profound impact through their dedication to empowering communities and individuals. Their work, particularly with the Iris Centre in Zimpeto, has fostered transformation by providing educational opportunities, healthcare, and spiritual guidance. They inspire hope and resilience, helping people overcome challenging circumstances and improve their quality of life. Their efforts have created lasting change, nurturing a sense of community and belonging. Through their compassion and commitment, the Lazars have played a significant part in transforming lives and have inspired others to participate in meaningful change as well. The Iris centre in Zimpeto continues to be a pivotal institution dedicated to supporting vulnerable children and families in the community."

Pastor Surprise Sithole
Author of *Voice in the Night*
Co-founder of *Iris Global*

"It is such an honour to endorse this book. I am so glad Steve and these youth have put pen to paper to share some of the incredible stories of God's grace and power that they've witnessed and been a part of in Mozambique.

From the plains of the Limpopo to the source of the Nile and beyond, Africa is a vast continent with multitudes of people who have experienced much suffering and difficulties. From the calamities of centuries-long slavery to today's struggles with wars, corruption, disease, and malnutrition, Africa's needs are overwhelming and urgent.

Across a world of distance, God called Steve and Ros Lazar to Mozambique, where they joined the remarkable work begun by Heidi and Rolland Baker in Maputo. Leaving behind the comforts of their beautiful home country of Australia, they stepped into a new world - one marked by hardship and pain, with communities displaced by war, families devastated by AIDS, and countless orphans.

Proverbs 25:25 says, "Like cold water to a weary soul is good news from a distant land." From the distant land of Australia, God brought the Lazars to the weary souls of Mozambique. Many have been refreshed and transformed by the good news of the Gospel through their ministry. With their hands to the plough, they have never looked back.

Steve and Ros have poured their lives into people who were rejected, forgotten, and deemed insignificant by worldly standards - yet deeply precious in the eyes of the Father. Moved solely by compassion and God's love, they have embraced the unloved and lived alongside them for nearly three decades. They've invested their resources, time, and energy to see these young ones grow up, rise above their circumstances, and fulfil their God-given potential as lives healed by Jesus.

This book is filled with unique and wonderful stories of lives touched and transformed by God's grace and the tireless work of many missionaries, pastors and visitors. May it stand as a testament to generations to come of what God can do... out of the dust."

Luís Cabral D.Min
Senior Pastor *Australia for Christ Church,* Australia

"Every story in this beautiful book will capture your heart and leave you in awe of our heavenly Father.

Out of the Dust by Steve Lazar brings together stories from their decades serving as true missionaries in Mozambique. Each one of us in the body of Christ will be encouraged as we read testimony after testimony of the love of Jesus rescuing the lost and forgotten of this world – our heavenly Father sees each one.

Thank you, Steve and Ros Lazar and Iris Global, for loving for a lifetime and answering the call. May we all heed this call to disciple the nations."

John Arnott
Founder *Catch the Fire* World and Toronto

Contents

Foreword by Heidi Baker 9
Preface 13
Acknowledgements 17
Introduction: Iris Global History 21

Stories of Hope

1. Augusto Lopes 43
2. Ana Zaida Munguambe 55
3. Alimo Pedro 67
4. Aniceta Martins 81
5. Armando Nguenha 87
6. Araújo Mapanzene 101
7. Beatriz Timane 107
8. César Senda 113
9. Alberto Nuvunga 117
10. Francisco Mandlate 127
11. Hermínio Muchave 137
12. Hilda Francisco 155
13. Jimia Guite 165
14. Joaneta Zitha 169
15. João Vasco Novela 175
16. Mónica Machel 185
17. Nhelety Mandlate 191
18. Rabia Senda 195
19. Ramos Macamo 201
20. Silavio Pedro 215
21. Sina Armando 227
22. Lourenço and Miguel Carimo 237
23. Ana Samu 245
24. Nilza Vincent 251
25. Felismina Almeida 257
26. It's all about Jesus 263

Meet the Author 269

FOREWORD

Heidi Baker

AFTER THIRTY YEARS in Mozambique, Rolland and I can safely say you don't meet missionaries like Steve and Ros Lazar very often. When we first welcomed them to Iris, we desperately needed more help — help with administration, help with ministry, help with emotional support, help with everything! We especially needed help running our children's center at Zimpeto, in the capital city of Maputo. There were countless children living on the streets and in the garbage dump, and since we wanted to take in everyone we possibly could, the job was always growing bigger. Every single day we were being stretched beyond our abilities. We didn't have much planned in advance, but we believed God would take care of us. As it turned out, one of the greatest things He did for us was to send Steve and Ros.

The first commitment they made to Iris was to stay for a year. Happily, for us, they didn't go home. It has been decades since then, and they've been with us at Iris ever since. Under their leadership Zimpeto has been a real oasis of warmth and discipleship. It would be impossible to describe everything they've gone through, or all the beautiful things they've done and seen, but we couldn't be happier to have shared their journey. The hardships have been frequent, but through it all Steve and Ros have remained two of the most genuinely tenacious and upbeat people we've ever met. I've watched them handle just about every kind of challenge with humility, and I'm continually impressed at how Steve always seems to come out of even the craziest situations with a peaceful solution. However dark or desperate things might seem (and they can seem desperate!) he is always able to make us laugh. That has been priceless.

Even more importantly, Steve and Ros always truly shared our heart to stop for the one in need. They always had a very special desire to get to know and love the individual child. We always preach that we don't need to fix the whole world, we just need to be willing to pay attention to the ones God places in front of us today. The ones he sends us to love here and now. That's what Steve and Ros have always done. I believe they're some of the greatest examples of this attitude you can find at Iris or anywhere else. In these pages you will read some of the powerful stories of the ones they stopped for.

The title of this book comes from Psalm 113:7-8: "He raises the poor from the dust and lifts the needy from the ash heap; he seats them with princes, with the princes of his people." Many of the people Steve records once owned nothing but what they could scavenge from heaps of burned refuse. God called Steve and Ros to them. They have given their whole lives to answer that call. But these are not stories about the generosity of westerners. These are the stories of young people who have given us more than we could ever give them. Their voices deserve to be heard, because one thing I can tell you after living beside them for so long is that these Mozambican brothers and sisters are the most resilient people I have ever come across on the planet. Many of them have been through the unimaginable yet came out on the other side filled with the grace that makes everything in life worthwhile. They might so easily have chosen bitterness, but they did not. They teach us about forgiveness. They teach us about hope. They teach us about pure faith. If you listen to them with an open heart, it seems almost impossible that you wouldn't be motivated to live with greater love, kindness, and mercy during each day that God gives you on this earth.

Many of the kids we began caring for at the beginning are soaring, with careers and families of their own. Others still struggle with the storms of life in a difficult nation, filled with its own dangers and temptations. We are praying for them always. Life expectancy remains shorter in Mozambique than in the west, and more than a few have already finished their race on earth. Truly, one of the greatest joys we look forward to in heaven is to meet them again. Our hope is sure. We know they are already enjoying a happiness we cannot yet imagine. Here in the world everything passes, but they have come into the riches of our Father's house. As you learn about their lives, we pray you too will be even more empowered by the love of God to stop for the one in need.

Dr. Heidi Baker
Co-Founder and Chairman of the Board, *Iris Global*

PREFACE

WHEN I TOLD my wife Ros I was writing a book, she suggested the title "A book written by a man who does not read."

I only remember twice having a significant dream. One was in 2008, when there were troubles on our base. As we thought and prayed as to our response, I dreamt about building a prayer room and eventually a new church. I woke the next morning and drew up plans, which we submitted to an architect. A year later, the prayer room was opened, and, in 2022, we completed and dedicated the new church.

A few times, friends suggested that Ros and I write a book about our experiences in Zimpeto. Then, in 2022, I dreamt about writing a book. The Lord immediately gave me the title and what the book was to be based on.

The title of this book comes from Psalm 113: 7-8, "He raises the poor from the dust and lifts the needy from the ash heap; he seats them with princes, with the princes of their people." Hence the title "Out of the Dust."

It has been a privilege and honour for Ros and me to be serving as volunteer missionaries at Iris Global Zimpeto (formally Iris Ministries) in Maputo, Mozambique, since 2001.

In a very poor country such as Mozambique, there are many aid organisations that regularly bring in food, clothing and supplies. There are also huge evangelism outreaches and crusades that bring the Gospel.

What attracted us to Iris Global is that they do both. They feed the hungry, clothe the naked, house the homeless, attend to the sick and at the same time share the good news of Jesus.

That's the Gospel in action. Jesus is the reward and the prize.

Initially, Ros and I went to Mozambique to serve for one year, and it has now been twenty-four. Missions and serving the poor is not a sprint - it is a marathon.

The reward of serving long-term is to see valuable fruit produced: hungry children fed, educated, healed, restored, ministered to and loved back to life.

This book is a collection of just a few of the stories of those children, now men and women, who are "running the race of life".

Revelation 12:11 says, "They triumphed over him by the blood of the Lamb and by the word of their testimony." The following chapters in this book are living stones to this scripture. Many of these lives were extremely difficult and traumatised. They had good reason to "give up". But because of Jesus and what He did on the cross, in their lives they have overcome.

The stories have been written or dictated by the young men and women themselves. The stories are their own words. Because of this, there are differences between the terms used by the authors when referring to various people. For example, the terms *Mana/Mano* and *Mama/Papa* are used interchangeably: both are ways of addressing people with respect and affection.

Similarly, in these stories, different authors use different names for people and organisations. For example, Ros is sometimes referred to as Mana Rosa, and Heidi as Mama Aida. As "Iris Ministries" later became "Iris Global", there are references to both names throughout the stories.

The authors have included details of their own choice - some with quite explicit descriptions of difficult seasons, others with a more general overview. Some stories are brief while others are longer. It was important that the story was theirs - not my interpretation or analysis. I have not corrected the form of the stories, to preserve their perspective.

These young men and women are now doing all the things we love to do in life: to get educated, marry, study, find a job, earn money, and serve God wherever they live in their community and area of influence.

Like the story of the raising of Lazarus, Jesus does the miracle, and we get to unwrap the grave clothes.

As I often say: the only difference between me and those we serve in Mozambique is where we were born.

Along with these printed stories, there are many other young people who are not "flying" - who were given the same opportunity, but did not take up the gifts and opportunities offered.

Some refused to go to school and did not study. Many did not accept help. As they left our base, they left Jesus at the front gate and lived lives of their own choice, but we were always there for them with a smile, a hug, a meal, clothing, and a prayer.

Then, there were those who came to the center sick, malnourished, and mistreated. We loved them into death - into the arms of Jesus. Thabo, Inacio, Helena, Naftal, Benedita, Jimmy, Percina, and Zulfa - a sample of those who passed too early into Heaven. These are just names to those who read this book, but to us (and to Jesus) they were precious children we loved with all our hearts. Truly, they are in a "better" place.

I remember clearly Helena, who came to us as a little girl. She was rejected by her family due to a chronic infection. In her 12 years with us, her great desire was to receive a visit and to be able to visit her family. Helena's family never visited but showed lots of emotions at her funeral. She passed away in hospital, of cerebral meningitis. Our children had prayed and prayed for her recovery, yet she died an excruciating death.

These very different outcomes (success, disappointment, tragedy, heartbreak) reflect the reality for those whose heart is to love like Jesus did. Yet we celebrate the successes: this helps us to deal with the inevitable difficulties along the way.

As John 16:33 says, "I have told you these things, so that in me you may have peace. In this world you will have trouble. But take heart! I have overcome the world."

This book celebrates the tenacity of those who had every reason to give up but who pressed ahead and are reaping a great reward. It celebrates their successes. Above all, it is a testimony to the amazing goodness of God.

ACKNOWLEDGEMENTS

As I look back on my life, there is so much to be thankful for.

Both Ros and I were raised in Christian households. Our parents brought us up in the ways of the Lord, which gave us a solid foundation to find our own way.

We thank God for giving us such wonderful opportunities throughout our lives to experience His goodness. We have sought to not just be "hearers" of His Word but "doers", as the scriptures encourage us to do. That obedience has taken us all over the world. Our journey has been a great joy.

Both Ros and I were touched in the charismatic movement that swept Australia in the 1970s and 1980s. We experienced a different aspect of God during these years.

A huge influence in our lives was being part of Spirit Alive Ministries (now the Australian Prayer Network). From 1984 until 1995, we joined intercessors all over Australia praying for cities, towns, churches and community leaders. We began to learn what it meant to live by faith and to be "totally available and radically obedient", as our leader Brian Pickering would remind us each month. Thanks to the APN for all you taught us.

While on teaching exchange in Toronto, Canada in 1995/96, we joined what was known as the "Renewal" at the Toronto Airport Christian Fellowship (now Catch the Fire). We fell in love with God the Father in a fresh and new way. Our whole family was touched, and this set us on the path towards missions. Thanks to John and Carol Arnott and Peter and Heather Jackson, who taught us about a loving God and Father. It was there we first heard Heidi and Rolland Baker (our founders) share.

We still return to the church in Toronto each year to soak up and remember and enjoy the deposit of God there.

Thanks to Heidi and Rolland who really modelled what it meant to be missionaries: loving the poor and sharing the Gospel. Thanks for trusting Ros and me enough to hand over the leadership of the Zimpeto base in 2003. We love and honour you both from the bottom of our hearts.

To our sending church - Vision Church in Canberra, Australia - who still, 25 years after our first visit, support us financially, prayerfully and by regularly sending teams: you are family and always welcome us "home" when in Australia. The founding pastors, Peter and Judy Thompson, encouraged us in our walk and pushed us forward into our destiny.

To our family, friends, churches and schools who have supported us, enabling us to be in Mozambique "comfortably" over these years - allowing us to not have to spend all our time worried over finances and provision. Thanks to many of you who have "stepped out of the boat" and visited us in Mozambique. Your generosity and love have sustained us.

To the many, many, missionaries who have served alongside us: thanks for leaving your families, homes, churches, culture and countries to serve God in Mozambique. There is no better place to be than where God wants you to be. As Heidi often says, "Stop for the One". You have truly done that - some for a year, others have been with us since the beginning. Thanks.

To our Mozambican pastors, leaders and workers who have stood with us: the fruit of your labour is the testimonies you read in this book. To the National Administrator of Iris Global, Francisco Mandlate - friend, mentor and wise man - we often said, "Francisco, if you leave, we are leaving!!" You are a pillar of strength, knowledge and wisdom.

To our family, who have sacrificed much: we have missed weddings, births, funerals and many family functions while serving. Thanks for understanding, loving us, always welcoming us "home"; for the many goodbye "plane letters" that brought tears to our eyes and for being there for us always.

To our children, Liz and Pete (and their families): our greatest joy has been you travelling part of this journey with us. Your years with us in Mozambique, your visits since then, and your unending support and passion for the poor has encouraged us and spurred us on. For many reasons you were not able to continue to journey with us.

To Ros, my wife: this is not a journey I would have liked to travel alone. Ros had the vision back in 1996 that this was time "to go". We have run together on this life's journey. Apart from floods, riots, lack of electricity, credit card scams, theft and many long flights, I have loved every minute with you. We are closer to the end than the beginning and I am truly a blessed man (even though my golf handicap has been adversely affected).

To those who helped edit and put this book together (Justin Hartley, Peter Moyle, Paul and Sally Cosgrove, Alexandra Cabral, Ros Lazar): many thanks (from a man who rarely reads a book). It was a great team effort.

INTRODUCTION
IRIS GLOBAL HISTORY
(Rolland Baker)

"HEIDI AND I began Iris Global (previously Iris Ministries) in 1980 and have been missionaries since then. We were both ordained as ministers in 1985 after completing our BA and MA degrees at Vanguard University in southern California. I majored in Biblical Studies, and Heidi in Communications and Church Leadership. I am a third-generation missionary born in China, and raised in China, Hong Kong and Taiwan. I was greatly influenced by my grandfather, H. A. Baker, who wrote "Visions Beyond the Veil," an account of the extended visions of heaven and hell that children received in his remote orphanage in southwest China two generations ago.

> "Blessed are the poor in spirit, for theirs is the kingdom of heaven." (Matthew 5:3)

Heidi was powerfully called to the mission field at age sixteen when she was living on an Indian reservation in Mississippi as an American Field Service student. Several months after she was led to Jesus by a Navajo evangelist, she was taken up in a vision for several hours and heard Jesus speak audibly to her and tell her to be a minister and a missionary to Africa, Asia, and England. When she returned home to Laguna Beach, California, she began ministering at every opportunity and leading short-term mission teams. We met at a small charismatic church in Dana Point and got married six months later after realizing we had the same radical desire to see revival among the poor and forgotten of the world.

We spent our first six years together leading evangelistic dance-drama teams all over Asia, making use of our backgrounds in creative media and the performing arts. But we increasingly came into intimate contact with the desperately poor and could no longer be satisfied by large meetings and quick visits to various locations, even though thousands were coming to Jesus. We had to learn to slow down and take care of long-term needs, one person at a time.

We began by working with the poor in the slums of central Jakarta, Indonesia, and then among the forgotten street-sleepers and elderly in the most crowded urban area in the world, central Kowloon in Hong Kong. Jackie Pullinger's work among drug addicts in the Walled City was a major influence in our lives.

In 1992 we left Asia to do our PhDs in systematic theology at King's College, University of London. But we couldn't stop ministering to the poor, and so at the same time we planted a warm and thriving church community for the homeless of downtown London, joined by a kaleidoscope of students, lawyers, businesspeople and friends from many countries. We learned the composite beauty of the Body of Christ!

For years we longed to get to Africa in fulfillment of our calling to prove the Gospel in the most challenging situation we could find. We wanted to see a continuation of "Visions Beyond the Veil," and believed with my grandfather that the most likely place to see such revival again was among the most unlikely! So, we were drawn to Mozambique, officially listed at the time as the poorest country in the world.

A few days into my initial visit to Maputo, Mozambique's capital, I was offered an orphanage at Chihango that no one would support, not even large churches in South Africa or European donor nations. It was horribly dilapidated, with eighty miserable, neglected children in rags. I thought it was a perfect test of the Sermon on the Mount. Our Father in heaven knows what we need. Seek first His Kingdom and righteousness, and these things will be ours as well ... Take no thought for tomorrow. Why worry? Jesus is enough for us, for anyone.

Alone and without support, Heidi and I offered to take over the Chihango center. We were thrilled for the opportunity to bring the Gospel there. Within months, most of the children came to Jesus and were filled with the Holy Spirit, weeping, while still in rags, with gratitude for their salvation. Jesus provided miraculously, more all the time as our children prayed night and day for their daily food. We brought in teams, improved the centre, and took some of the children to the streets to share with other street children what God had done for them. Some were lost in visions, taken to heaven and danced around the throne of God on the shoulders of angels.

But abruptly, when the center had grown to over three hundred children, we were evicted. Totally without a back-up plan, our children marched off down the road without a home, many barefoot. We lost everything.

But we were only beginning to taste the power of God in Mozambique!"

Always Enough

Iris was donated undeveloped land in the nearby town of Machava by sympathetic officials. Some old army tents – and one big circus tent – were provided, and practically overnight a new village of children sprang up where a week before there had been only grass and trees. It was even more basic than Chihango had been, but it would do for the time being, and everyone was overjoyed. Iris's little community had prayed long and hard for water, both in spirit and in the natural. Very soon, a new well was dug at Machava, yielding fresh, clean water. Iris now had an abundance of both kinds of water.

By the end of its third year in Mozambique, Iris had acquired and lost one major centre, begun a new base from the dirt up in Machava, and purchased land at Zimpeto, an outlying district of Maputo. Zimpeto lay at the outskirts of the capital, close to what Heidi calls one of her favorite churches: the "bocaria," Maputo's largest dump, where crowds of the poor scavenged mountains of trash for a scant living. Some of the great miracles Iris has witnessed occurred there. Many circumstances at this time remained difficult, but all the most bitter setbacks – of which there were many more than can be told – were more than offset by extraordinary wonders and the manifest presence of God.

One such event, which has permanently shaped the values of Iris, occurred when Heidi, exhausted amid the Chihango struggles, flew out to a Christian renewal conference in North America. She was in especially desperate need of renewal, exhausted by the work and the responsibility for over three hundred children who called her "Mama Aida." Finances were tight. Two doctors had just told her she absolutely could not make the trip because she had a serious case of double pneumonia and blood poisoning. But being stubborn in faith and spirit, she boarded a plane anyway and flew more than thirty hours to the conference.

At the very start of the event God opened her lungs and allowed her to breathe freely. Each day after, amid constant worship, teaching and prayer, her strength increased. She spent many hours receiving prayer from loving people on the ministry team. Heidi often tells of finding it difficult to be still and receive after years of ministry, but this soon became a deeply healing time for her.

Heidi writes: One night I was groaning in intercession for the children of Mozambique. There were thousands coming toward me, and I was crying, "No, Lord. There are too many!" Then I had a dramatic, clear vision of Jesus. I was with Him, and thousands and thousands of children surrounded us. I saw His shining face, and His intense, burning eyes of love. I also saw His body. It was bruised and broken, and His side was pierced. He said, "Look into My eyes. You give them something to eat." Then, He took a piece of His broken body and handed it to me. It became bread in my hands, and I began to give it to the children. It multiplied in my hands. Then again, the Lord said, "Look into My eyes. You give them something to drink." He gave me a cup of blood and water, which flowed from his side. I knew it was a cup of suffering and joy. I drank it and then began to give it to the children to drink. The cup did not go dry. By this point I was crying uncontrollably. I was completely undone by His fiery eyes of love. I realized what it had cost Him to provide such spiritual and physical food for us all. The Lord spoke to my heart and said, "There will always be enough, because I died."

Ever since, one of the absolute core principles of Iris has been to offer a home to any child found in Mozambique without a family, regardless of financial or other considerations. The numbers grow. Today Rolland and Heidi cry out for a continuation of the visitation of God experienced by the children of H.A. Baker's children's centre in China long ago. More testimonies are now accumulating than can be written – but the great story of this rising generation of children is just beginning.

Growth and Current Events

Iris experienced explosive growth throughout the late 1990s and 2000s. As more and more children found a home in Iris, and more outreaches brought multitudes to the Lord, people began asking Iris for pastoral training. Pastors long isolated in the countryside requested "bush conferences," and when they occurred people would often walk for days to gather at them. Hundreds, then thousands of new churches sprang up, and many old ones became affiliated with Iris. In the West many began to hear about events in Mozambique, and Rolland and Heidi were invited to speak in nations around the globe. Foreign volunteers came in increasing numbers.

When Mozambique was rocked by catastrophic flooding in 2000 and again in 2001, Iris's far-reaching network of rural churches became an effective arm of relief. It was a terrible time, and despite a sudden influx of international aid, hundreds of thousands were displaced and suffered greatly with hunger, disease and loss of life. Iris, however, was positioned to work extensively in the temporary refugee camps and was able to feed many thousands beyond its usual numbers. There was also desperate spiritual hunger among battered survivors, and a great outpouring of the Spirit fell upon them. Most international attention moved away quickly, but Iris remained, with many more to care for, physically and spiritually.

Children's schools (including several of the top-ranked schools in the country), Bible schools and clinics began to open under Iris. An international school for missionaries opened in the mid-2000s. When the Zimpeto children's centre had been moderately well-established, Rolland and Heidi left it in the capable hands of Steve and Ros Lazar from Australia and moved permanently to Pemba in 2004. A coast city in the far north of Mozambique, Pemba was surrounded by unreached tribal groups with syncretistic beliefs. Almost every outreach to a village resulted in a new church, usually catalyzed by miraculous healings. Today the "unreached" of these tribes are fast dwindling.

As churches swelled and community outreaches multiplied, Iris began to expand into other nations, opening bases in similar ways. As of this writing, Iris is active in thirty-four nations and is still growing. As expansion has proceeded far faster than all initial expectations, Iris is hard at work to develop effective, Spirit-led new organisational capacities to serve the movement.

Our progress thus far has been entirely miraculous: all told, Iris Global currently feeds well over 10,000 children a day, as well as various members of many other communities. Its network of churches also numbers in the thousands. Iris operates three Bible schools, in addition to its three primary schools and its Harvest School of Missions. Current major projects include continuing outreaches to very remote coastal regions, strategic use of its bush aircraft, investment in a range of cottage industries, and a well-drilling operation that transforms life in desperately dry villages. Many more projects are under consideration. National leaders are rising with wisdom and power, and many new nations beckon beyond. We believe that the best is yet to come.

We value immediate intimacy with Jesus, a life of utterly needed miracles, concentration on the humble and lowly, willingness to suffer if necessary, and the unquenchable joy of the Lord, which is our energy, motivation, weapon and reward, and not optional!

May the Word of God spread in power to the remote corners of the world, and may the poor, the crippled, the lame and the blind, people who have never tasted the goodness of God, be drawn to the King's great banquet!

Outreach in Pemba – Steve, Heidi and Rolland

Iris Global leaders: Pastor José Novela, Steve & Ros Lazar, Francisco Mandlate, Tony & Pamela Maxwell, Rolland Baker, Pastor Surprise and Triphena Sithole

| Introduction | 29

Steve and Ros Lazar History

Until 2000, I was a School Director and Mathematics teacher, having taught in Australia, New Zealand and Canada for more than 20 years. Ros is a Registered Nurse specialising in paediatrics. We were married in 1981 and have two children, Peter and Elizabeth.

As a young child, Ros watched the movie of the life of Gladys Aylward, "The Inn of the Sixth Happiness". From then, within Ros grew a desire to work with vulnerable children and one day serve on the mission field.

While teaching in Canada during 1995 and 1996, the Toronto Airport Christian Fellowship (now Catch the Fire Church) became our "home church". During a conference at the church, we heard Rolland and Heidi Baker share about the work they were doing on the streets of Maputo, Mozambique - the sixth poorest country in the world. They were rescuing orphans and vulnerable children from severe poverty and mistreatment, caring for them and loving them back to life.

We knew God was speaking to us through the Bakers' testimony they shared at the Toronto church. We knew enough about God to know when He speaks to our hearts, we must do something about it. From that night, we began communicating with and supporting the work of Iris Ministries (now Iris Global) and Rolland and Heidi Baker.

Ros and I were interested in "serving God and giving opportunity to others less fortunate than us". Both Ros and I love children. In December 1999, we spent our school holidays visiting mission bases in Thailand and Mozambique. We visited the Zimpeto base in Maputo for ten days. After returning from Mozambique and Thailand, we asked God where were we most needed. Clearly, He responded: in Maputo, at the Zimpeto base. We then took three months leave from our work in Australia in mid 2000, to visit Zimpeto again.

In 2001, we had enough funds and faith to volunteer in Zimpeto for one year. We fell so in love with the children and the community in Zimpeto that we stepped out in faith, and one year became two, and then three. As of 2024, we have been there for twenty-four years. We are still volunteers: supported by family, friends, and several churches.

Beginning full time in 2001, Ros and I worked alongside Rolland and Heidi, until 2003, when the Bakers began the move to Pemba, the capital city of the Northern province Cabo Delgado.

At this time, Rolland and Heidi asked us to lead the base in Zimpeto. In 2003, there were more than 500 children living on the base: children from the streets and garbage dump; children who were orphaned, abandoned and sick. As we began serving in Zimpeto, God gave Ros and me a vision. It was twofold - to care for children, and to raise up national leaders.

From 2001 until late 2019, Ros and I were full-time in Mozambique. We lived there with our two children and sought to model family to children who came from dysfunctional backgrounds.

We built a house and spent our days overseeing the base, caring for the community, opening and establishing the clinic, developing the school, and supporting the church.

In 2002, during a medical crisis on the base, Ros and I took ten of the most vulnerable babies into our house to protect them. When the crisis passed, those ten children remained with us for the following years - the last of them moving to the community in 2019. Ernesto, Ângelo, Joaneta, Luís, Gito, Jimmy, Percina, Lija, Ivan and, later, Crimelda and João, called our house their home.

We schooled them, cared for them, loved them and nursed them to health. We never adopted them, but they had a special place in our hearts (and still do). Each of them has their own story and we are proud of them all. Some of them are studying at university, some have their own families, most of them are still serving God in the church. Along the journey, two of the youth - Jimmy and Percina - passed away.

Major events on the base during our time there have included the building of a purpose-built prayer room (opened in 2009), construction of a new church (officially opened in 2022), construction of an academic school for 1500 students, renovating new accommodation for those living on the base (including completely pulling down and rebuilding the girls' area), accommodating and providing ministry opportunities for 400 visitors a year, and encouraging community care and church growth.

At Christmas of 2019, Ros and I headed back to Australia for three months rest. When Covid hit we were locked within the borders of Australia until mid 2022.

At the time of leaving for Australia in December 2019, we appointed Augusto and Clara Lopes as Directors of Operations. Augusto is one of the original boys who came to Zimpeto (you will find his testimony in this book). He is now a qualified Engineer and is completing his Master's. Clara is a passionate missionary currently completing her degree in Psychology. Little did we know at that time we would be away for more than two years. God knew. They are the future leaders of the base.

In 2022, Ros was awarded the Order of Australia Medal for services to Mozambique. This is the highest community award given in Australia. It is rare to be given towards foreign work or to Christian based care. Ros accepted the Award, she says, "for both of us" in recognition of our combined contribution to Mozambique.

In 2024, we invited Herminio Muchave and his wife Kasey to return to Zimpeto to take on the role of Children's Director. As you will read, Herminio was also a child at the centre and you will find his testimony later in this book.

I mentioned above that God gave us a vision: to care for children and raise up national leaders. In the last twenty-four years we have cared for, loved, reunited with families, and educated several hundred children. This is our great joy. The second part of our vision is also almost complete. In 2003, all our area leaders were foreign missionaries. Twenty-one years later, almost all areas are now in the hands of – and overseen by – Godly, educated, loving Mozambicans. Many of them grew up on the base.

It is true to say - our ceiling is their floor.

So why have we given our lives to this endeavour? We love the Lord, and we love to help those who live in need. The Bible says that the purest form of religion is to minister to "orphans and widows". Those whom we support want the same thing as our own families - education, health care, housing, and family life. We help them do this.

At the time of writing, Mozambique is one of the ten poorest countries in the world. Compared with 2003, there is now a better and more regulated supporting infrastructure, including Social Services.

Our goal is to bring referred children into the centre for a period, during which we aim to maintain contact with their families, attend to the health and emotional issues of the children, obtain a place for them in the medical system if needed, educate them, protect them, and strengthen the families in order to reunite the children with them.

There are ten foreign volunteers, and 150 full- and part-time Mozambican staff.

The base serves not only the needs of our resident children but also the poorest of the poor from the surrounding areas. Here, the impossible happens! We join with the people of Mozambique to believe for a bright, joy-filled and prosperous future.

Our joy is to love each one in front of us, to raise healthy children, to reunite families, and to support the poor in the community around us in every way we can.

The base covers 10 acres, and includes a Nursery, Baby House, residential care for children and youth (both boys and girls), a Special Needs programme, morning and afternoon schools (for 1,500 students), a community clinic, library and computing centre. We run outreaches to the garbage dump, streets and the local community, where we feed and care for hundreds of people. We build houses, provide electricity and water, and give places in our school for children to be educated. We offer spiritual growth in our church - which is large and active - and through the churches in the community. We have between two and three hundred visitors a year, and would love to hear from you if you're interested in partnering with us in this exciting journey.

More information can be found at www.irisglobal.org or on the Zimpeto website: www.irisminzimpeto.org

The Mozambican Government does not provide financial support. However, each area of the ministry is licenced and works under the authority of the appropriate government department. The school is registered under the Department of Education, the clinic under the Ministry of Health, our workers under the Ministry of Works, the church and Bible school under the Ministry of Religion, and our foreign workers under the Ministry of Foreign Affairs.

These departments regularly make visits and inspections of the centre and occasionally use our base as a model for other institutions of how to care for orphans and vulnerable children.

Our funding comes purely from donations: hundreds of generous churches, families, friends, organisations and individuals join in to sustain this incredible work.

Footnotes:

Since 2006, every child entering the centre has been thoroughly investigated by the Social Welfare team. Iris Global Zimpeto believe that the family is the basic building block of society. Family is the safe community wherein children are loved, nurtured, grow and learn. Although poverty is not a sufficient reason to separate a child from their family, sometimes the family unit is in crisis and unable to provide adequate care for the child to grow.

Iris Global Zimpeto aims to provide a temporary, safe place for a child, while strengthening the family unit. Support for a family may include a food box, house construction, education, medical assistance, employment and small business opportunity. While the child is accommodated in the centre, communication is maintained with the family. After review by the Social Welfare team, when a family is ready, a child will be reintegrated. Since 2001 hundreds of children have been successfully reintegrated with their family, with ongoing support if needed.

New church building

School church service

Intercession in the prayer room

Children's Day 2024 - the baby house

Special Needs house - Children's Day 2024

Introduction | 39

Some of the youth from Steve & Ros Lazar's house - Crimelda, Gito, Ângelo, Joaneta, Luís, Lija, Ernesto, Ivan

Same youth -10 years later

Son Peter, his wife Trish, and grandson Henry

Daughter Liz, with grandchildren Lena and Bella

CHAPTER 1

Augusto Lopes

It is a great honour for me to share my story as a part of this book. I have never shared my full testimony with the details I will share here. It is hard for me to think about my past because it causes me a lot of pain. Yet I feel that God is providing me an opportunity of healing through this writing. My story and testimony are to glorify our almighty God and to understand how God sees our future. He sees good things where no one else can.

My journey starts in June 1987, when I was born in the capital city Maputo. In total we were twelve siblings, but most of them died, and now we are just four. Without knowing all the background reasons, many of my siblings suffered and died because of poverty. When the last two died, I understood clearly how hard life was for my family.

My father passed away within a few months of me being born and life for our family started to be very hard. My mother could not feed us, and she did not have any skill to be able to work. She could not help the family as my father had been the provider, and everything was very difficult.

At the same time, we lost our house. That meant we did not have a place to live. Our uncle sent us away from our home saying that the house did not belong to our family but to his. This caused lots of confusion, and that was the beginning of the separation of our family. My mother left us behind and went to the bush to try to find a place to live. She began a small garden plot to produce some vegetables to feed us. This was an extremely difficult time because the country was in a state of civil war. We had to live on the streets. Life was very basic.

My sister got involved with prostitution to survive, and she just disappeared. She got lost in that terrible life - and this was a time when there was severe hunger in Mozambique. When my mother heard about my sister, she came back to try to help, but the lack of food was too much.

A few years later, my older brother and I were living with another older sister in a house where there was great conflict, but then it was destroyed and unsafe to live in. We had to live on the streets again. We spent all the time on the street and often slept there. We tried to survive by picking up left-over food from trash bins and collecting coconuts at the markets to eat them as a meal.

The hardest part of this traumatic experience was when my brother and I saw an eight-year-old child being hit by a car. She died trying to save a coconut that was placed on the road. (The coconuts were very hard and so were placed in the middle of the road. When a car passed by and ran over the coconut, we would run onto the road to retrieve it.) But as this little girl ran to retrieve the crushed coconut a second car ran over her.

We were all so scared and stopped going to the street for two days, but we did not have any other options as we were hungry. We then heard about a family member that was living in a Maputo area called Maxaquene, and we thought maybe we could stay there. We walked ten kilometres to get there, but then my brother disappeared and left me there.

I attempted to find my way back, but I got lost and I was crying a lot. I believe that God was watching me. At the end of that day, a lady found me and took me to her house. To be honest that was the best day of my life as I had a good shower and a very good meal. It was a "real family". I was in a strange place but happy. Unfortunately, my happiness was just for one day as the next morning she took me to the police station which was close to my house. I then found my brother again.

My sister returned home sick

A few years later, the war was almost finished. My mother came back to collect all of us to live in the bush with her, and that place was called Mulotana (about an hour outside of the capital city Maputo). We were the only family there, and we had to walk 3 to 5 km to find a neighbour. It was the end of one problem and the beginning of another.

In Mulotana there was no water, no school, no hospital, and no house. Our small hut was made of grass, and during rainy weather we could not sleep. I remember that there was a very old and abandoned construction site close to our house, and we used to go to sleep there in the rain. Sometimes we woke up in the middle of the night to run to that building because of rain. At times there were more than three families in that same place.

None of my siblings wanted to go with my mother to Mulotana; only me and my brother. About a year later, my sister (who was involved in prostitution) came to stay with us, because she was very sick with HIV and tuberculosis. She ended up passing away.

She passed away at the hospital. It had been a challenge for my mother to afford for her to go to hospital and to visit her there, but it was much more difficult to take her out of hospital for her funeral. We did not have a chance to bury my sister properly. Sadly, she was buried in a mass grave (which is a great shame and insult to the family. Mass burials are for people with no family or money and bodies are collected weekly and dumped without a burial ceremony, which is very important to families in Mozambique).

I started to go to a "school" which was under a tree. There were no teachers because they had to come from the city, and there was no transport. At this time, the roads were very poor.

I was happy to be living with a part of my family, but we were still struggling with life. We did not have school materials or uniforms, and it meant that my mother was not able to afford a proper education for us.

In that situation I was given up for adoption a couple of times. This did not go well. I just wanted someone to care for me and give me opportunity to study. All these families gave up on me and I ended up going back home.

I never understood why these other families gave up on me. I was only nine years old, but I felt I now had to work for myself to help my family. I used to collect fruit and vegetables in the bush, as well as tree branches to let them dry and make brooms. After collecting things, I had to walk 30km carrying brooms and vegetables on my head to sell them in the city.

During this time, my mother introduced me to a lady who used to buy brooms from her. My mother asked if I would work for her, selling products in the market. For my mother this was a chance for me to study because the lady wanted me to move to her house, which was in the city, where I could go to a school. At that time, I was about 11 years old.

We all saw that it was a chance for me to have a different life, but I had to work very hard for her. This was a condition of me going to live with her family. I was very happy because for the first time I was going to have a chance to live in a house with electricity and be able to watch TV.

Finally, my big day arrived as I moved to that house. I was

excited to be there. I was also very sad because I knew that my family was still suffering. Even at this age I had a clear understanding of the situation that my family was in.

It was a big step for me, but I did not have time for anything, because in the morning I was at school and in the afternoon at the market. I was so tired by the end of the day that I just wanted to sleep. I never had time to be a child. My salary was going to my mom to help with food for the family.

How I arrived at the Zimpeto centre

All was going well until I broke my leg one day playing football. I did not tell anyone, yet I was in great pain. On the first day it seemed like all was normal but the next day I could not walk. For a few days, I tried to hide that there was a problem. This was easy enough for me because no one used to pay any attention to me. I knew how to be responsible for myself and could go to school without any outside help.

Believe me, this was God's protection, even though it was before I knew Him. Deep down I felt His love.

So, for a few days I did not go to the school or market, but no one realised that, because no one cared for me. The only problem for them was that I was not bringing daily money from the market, and that's how they found that I was unwell.

My knee was very swollen, and I couldn't walk. The lady called my mother, and she came and took me to hospital. It was the beginning of a new journey, and it all happened very fast (it was just after the school tests at the end of 1999).

I really do not remember if I had an infection or not, but recovery was a very long process. I believe that God was saying it was time for me to lose everything, to gain new things.

As I was responsible for myself, I could not register myself at school for the following year (2000). I could not work anymore for the lady for at least a few months, so I was of no use to her. She had to find someone else to replace me. She wanted to send me back to my mother, but it wasn't possible at this time because of the floods.

It was raining a lot, and all the country started to have problems with floods. That gave me some time. My family was struggling with their lives, and our house made of bamboo and straw was destroyed by the rain. The lady felt that she needed to do something because it wasn't possible for me to return to my mother without a house as I would be there again in the bush without studying.

To be honest I felt there was no future for me and for my family. I did not know what would happen, but the only thing I knew is that my time with my family and with the lady was finished.

One of the daughters of that lady was working at Iris Ministries in Zimpeto, as a teacher. She told my mother that there was an institution there that took care of street children, and maybe they would accept me. My mother came and dropped me off at Zimpeto. At that time there were no regulations with Social Welfare. I was taken in without a problem, and someone took me to the dormitory. It was April 2000, and I was about to turn twelve years old.

Living at Zimpeto

I arrived at the centre very skinny, and I still had a big problem with my leg. I did not look like a normal child. At that time, it was not easy to be at the centre as there were more than 500 children, with most of them coming from the street.

To be honest, being at the centre was a challenge for many children but for me it was paradise. I had three meals a day and water for showers, without walking a long way to carry it.

I started to participate in real church for the first time and I received the first Christmas gift I had ever had in my life. This is why I love Christmas even today. It is not the same with other special days. I really do not celebrate my birthday as I never celebrated it with my family. My wife makes a big fuss on my birthday, but it feels very strange.

I studied very hard at school because I felt like someone who I did not know (perhaps God) was giving me a chance to have a better life. I was not a brilliant student, but I did my best. I also started to work in the maintenance area of Iris Ministries and helped with construction of the church and many other buildings at the centre. I knew that my family was suffering, and I started to help my mother every month. I remember that I was just receiving 50 Mets ($1) per month for helping around the centre.

My dream was that one day, I would have a house and take care of my family. A few years later these things happened with the help of Iris Ministries. They built three houses in the community close to the base. I received my own block of land and a simple house of my own.

After that I studied to become an electrician, and I worked in the community wiring houses. One of the first houses I worked in was that of the centre pastor named Nico. His family had confidence enough in me to put electricity in his house. At the same time, I was promoted to be an electrician at the center which included controlling the generator and emergency call-outs. I earned enough money to pay for my driving licence. I started to be a driver at the centre and helped with emergency driving for the clinic.

I also worked as a "chefe" during the weekend, overseeing children in the dormitories, and finally I was promoted again, to help in Human Resources, where I was able to learn many things. I was helping as a youth and not as a regular worker. At the same time, I was admitted to Eduardo Mondlane University to study Electrical Engineering. This was in 2011 just after I got married in Brazil to Clara. Together, we served God in this Ministry.

Despite all these blessings, my family was still struggling with life. I was doing my best to take care of my new wife but also continuing to support my mother and siblings.

Wedding story

One of the most important parts of my story is when I meet my wife Clara in 2009. She came from Brazil as a missionary to serve at the Zimpeto base. I was helping with youth in one of the dormitories, and Clara was directed to work with me. For me it was a dream come true. We met and prayed together for nine months before dating. After that with blessings from our parents, our base leaders Steve and Ros, and our leaders from Brazil, we got married.

It was a great honour. We got married in Brazil in August 2011, with the special presence of Steve and Ros representing my parents. Papa Steve and Mana Ros are a very important part of my life, from my education until my marriage. I am glad for their input into my life. They were the only family at my wedding in Brazil.

This was the beginning of my new family. My wife and I have been together now for thirteen years.

In 2014, Clara and I started a church in a very poor community where I lived in the past. In the beginning we were just supporting the widows and orphans, but now we are serving the Lord there. We are leading a small church. A great joy for me in 2010 was to baptise Clara.

In 2011, I felt like I failed in my mission to help my family. My older brother went through a very difficult situation, and he ended up committing suicide. He wrote a letter asking me to take care of his son, and he drank poison. I received a call to bring him to hospital in the middle of the night.

He was not a Christian, but God gave him three months before he died, and we introduced him to Jesus. He accepted Jesus as his Lord and Saviour.

Job decision

My dream was to finish my university course and find a job. In 2018, I graduated from university, and I started the journey of searching for a job. The centre directors, Steve and Ros Lazar, offered me a job to work with the finance team in Zimpeto. I did it for a month, but my dream was to work as an engineer. So, I decided to stop with working with the finance team, and I went to work in Matola as a trainee in Electrical Engineering. After two months of internship, I was called to CDM (the largest beer company in Mozambique) to work as an engineer. That was a wonderful opportunity for me. The salary was good, and the work conditions were excellent. It was like a dream come true.

My wife and I were very excited with my new job, but I also felt called to help at the Zimpeto center. I loved working directly with the children there. While I was offered the job at CDM, I received an offer to be the Director of Operations at Zimpeto. It was hard for me to decide what to do. Yet I knew that God was calling me back home to help the children.

After a few nights of prayers and thinking, I realised that God was giving me an opportunity to choose, and He would bless me anyway. Then finally I made the decision.

In 2019, my wife and I decided to accept the challenge of serving God at Zimpeto. I had to resign my contract at CDM. Many people did not understand my decision, but I had peace. God used people to take care of me, and now He was giving me a chance to impact and help someone else's life, the same way I was impacted and blessed during my formative years.

I am very glad about what God did for me through my leaders - Papa Steve and Mana Ros, and all the missionaries, and educators. I am who I am today because of Iris Ministries. I became this man because of God's touch on my life through this ministry. I am the first person in my family with a degree. I was rescued from the dust to sit with the kings and princes.

Looking back, I can see that God was preparing me for this moment. He gave me an opportunity to serve Him as the Director of Operations in the Zimpeto base.

Today my biological family and I are moving ahead. All the children in my family are studying. I am helping my sister with her university. I thank God for raising people with vision like Heidi and Rolland Baker, and Steve and Ros Lazar because they know all the steps I took to get to where I am today.

Thanks for being a part of my life. God used you all in a way that you cannot imagine. You brought some sunshine; some hope not just for me but for many others.

Thank you so much and God bless you all.

Augusto

Augusto 2003 -with Pascoal

Stories of Hope | 53

Augusto and Clara

Augusto and his family

Augusto and Clara with Steve and Ros - wedding day 2011

CHAPTER 2

Ana Zaida Munguambe

My name is Ana Zaida Mahiele Munguambe. I am 48 years old.

I am Mozambican, and was born in a small town called Zongoene in the province of Gaza. When I was born, my parents were married and had six children. My childhood was filled with lots of violence. My parents fought every day, and every time they fought, they physically attacked each other. Because of this my mother took us to my grandparents' house. Without delay my father came to apologize and we went back to our home. This situation did not make me comfortable. Despite having a good mother, my brothers and I were afraid of our father.

In 1984, I entered school to study. I really wanted to study, and my teachers thought I was very intelligent and that I had a bright future ahead of me.

As my parents had a lot of fights there came a time when my father abandoned the family and went to marry another woman with whom he had three children. At that moment we had my mother's full attention. She was a very hard-working woman. Even during the civil war that lasted 16 years, she never allowed us to go hungry. There were several times when she risked her own life to be able to bring bread into the house. I confess that even though my father was not present in my children's lives I missed him a lot. When my colleagues talked about something involving their parents, I felt very sad. I tried to understand the reason why my father would have abandoned us. My mother always tried to tell us that he might have his flaws, but he was a good father.

In 1992, I asked my parents to reconcile because we needed both of them together. They talked and came to an agreement. My father returned home, even though he had another family, and my mother accepted him.

Everything seemed to be going well until one day my father physically attacked my mother. She was hospitalized for 9 days in a provincial hospital in the city of Xai-Xai. This situation left me very confused, and I felt a sense of guilt. I was the one who had asked my parents to forgive each other and now my mother was here in a hospital bed. All I needed at that time was for my mother to be healed and to separate from my father. When she left the hospital alive, I said to her that I was not ready to lose her. I asked my Mum to separate from my father. I was very hurt by my father and wanted to get away from him. That is how my parents separated, and my mother began to assume both roles of father and mother at the same time. It was not easy, as it was a period of war. We were constantly running away from armed bandits: yet my mother always did her best to take care of her children.

About Education

Regarding education, I was a very diligent child at school but the area where I was born did not have a secondary school. After completing primary education, students had to move to the city to continue their studies. It was in this context that my older sister went to study in the city and became pregnant by one other classmates. I had thought that I would also continue my studies in the city. My father was very angry with this situation with my sister and decided that none of his daughters would continue studying as it was a waste of time to invest in a girl's education because they would come back pregnant. This situation affected me a lot. I went into depression. At the time I did not even know it was depression, but now I understand. I was finishing the 5th grade and the following year I had planned to study in the city, but now everything had ended.

Whenever my parents were together, my father made the decisions and my mother could not do anything. I wanted to continue studying. I went without eating for a week to see if my father would change his mind, but he didn't. I ran away from home, and I spent a week in the woods. My family looked for me and found me. I tried to commit suicide. I did not die, as my Mum took me to the hospital, and I was fine. The attempted suicide left my mother so worried that she decided to seek support, so that I could study. She took me to the city and talked to the midwife who helped her when I was born. She told her that I had tried to kill myself because I wanted to study. That is when the midwife looked for a boarding school that paid for me to stay and study. It was in this school where I studied 6th and 7th classes.

At that time, I wanted to continue my studies at the Chókwe Agricultural School, but due to the war that was intensifying, it was not possible. I had to return home. I felt that I had advanced a little but the desire to continue with my studies was enormous. At home there was nothing to do. During this period, we often had to hide in the bush because of armed bandits.

We were just subsistence farming. At a certain point I accepted that life would be like this, and I dedicated myself to this life. Education within my family had taken a different direction. For a woman to be married, you had to be good at farming and doing housework. I was being trained so that in the future I would be a good wife and a good mother. I did not like the idea but I did not have many alternatives.

About Marriage

When it comes to marriage, I have a lot to say. I grew up in an area where marriages were arranged by family members. In my house it was normal for people to come and ask me to be their son's wife without that son having even spoken to me. I found this situation very sad, and I did not agree with it.

I resisted until I was 17. That is when my aunts called a meeting to discuss the issue of me not agreeing to marriage. They asked why I did not agree to it. I explained that I was afraid of everything. I knew many girls who grew up with me who already had husbands, and the life they led was very sad. Everything was limited to going to the farm, taking care of the house, and having children. The husband could have many other women, to the point of bringing some to live in the same house. I found this situation very shameful, so I told them that I *would* perhaps get married there, in my area of origin, if it was to a city boy. I said this without realizing that they were determined to find me a husband.

In a short time, they had found me a boyfriend from the city who I didn't even know. They organized everything for me to meet the young man. They said it was time for me to get married because all the girls my age had done this. In a short time, the young man organised everything, and went to introduce himself to my family. He would pay the lobolo (dowry) to my family, and then they would accompany me to his house. I did not have many options. It was either agree to go with him or be kicked out of the house. My mother could not defend me. When she tried to say something, my father said that in his house, he alone could decide.

Four months passed while the groom was preparing to pay the dowry. That is when his sister suddenly came to my house to tell me that my future husband was sick and had been admitted to the hospital. She said that it was my obligation to take care of him. I tried to deny it, but to no avail. My parents ordered me to go to his house. Imagine suddenly you find yourself in the house of a strange person who you have never dated. You know nothing about this person, and he already calls you his wife.

I had a very bitter experience. He did actually have health problems, but I believe he took advantage of this situation, so I could care for him until he left the hospital. I said that I was preparing to join my family and that I would only stay another week, until he recovered. It was during this period that I became pregnant. This was two days before returning to my parents' house.

This was my first relationship. I did not understand much. I fell ill, so my family took me to the hospital where a simple test revealed that I was pregnant. I cried bitterly, but I could not change that situation. My family remained silent and no one tried to find out why I wasn't coming home. In a short time, I discovered that my life had now taken a different direction.

This man was no different from my father. He drank alcohol, smoked, beat me when I was pregnant, and brought women and slept with them inside the house where we lived. I went into shock. I was not prepared for this situation, and it was the greatest humiliation a woman could go through. At least I interpreted it that way. There were several attacks until one day I decided to register the case with the police, and they did nothing because he had a brother who was a police commander. I decided to go home alone.

To my surprise, my family welcomed me and didn't even ask why it took me so long. When I got home, I decided to hide the pregnancy, because I knew that if my parents found out they would send me back to his house and I didn't want to go. I managed to hide my belly until I was 7 months pregnant, but then they found out. I begged them to let me stay: I didn't want to go back. I stayed until the birth, and my boyfriend never came to visit me.

I assumed that I was now a single mother, and I had support from my own mother. I decided to look for work. I had some advantage because I knew how to read and write. I went to ask for work in a hotel that was still under construction. They asked what I knew how to do, because I did not have any documents. I replied that I knew how to do whatever they told me to do! The Human Resources technician asked why I wanted to work. I explained what had happened to me and he helped me get the job.

By the grace of God the owners of this hotel were Christians. It was with this work that I managed to organize my life and take care of my son. At a certain point I started to realize that my son had a health problem, but I did not know what it was. I often had to take him to the hospital. A few years passed and I met a boy and we started a relationship. It seemed like everything was going to work out. I got pregnant and had a second son.

At a certain point I discovered that my boyfriend was married and had four children. Yet I also already had a baby in my arms. In short, there was no chance of him marrying me, so I thought there must be something wrong with me.

In 1999, my eldest son's situation became complicated. He had a blood transfusion. Due to a mistake by the doctors he received blood that was not from his blood group. He fell sick and his belly started to grow. I took him to the hospital again and they discovered that the blood he received was not from his blood group, so it did not circulate through his veins, and it created clots. I did not know what to do. My mother came to help me and the boy received an injection to break up the blood clots. Unfortunately for me, the blood started to come out of his mouth, nostrils and anus. It came out of all channels, even his ears. My son lost his life in this situation. It was very difficult. I tried to find the reason for this misfortune but I couldn't find any answer. I cried a lot. At the same time, I realised that my other son was not in good health, but I did not understand what was wrong.

It was this same year that I was evangelised by my mother, who was already saved and following Jesus. She went to a small church that had just started, and sometimes she came to a conference in Maputo. One day I agreed to go to church with her. I started reading the Bible that she gave me, and God began to reveal Himself to me.

About my Salvation

I accepted Jesus as my Lord and Saviour in 1999, the same year when I was very distressed about the loss of my son. All I wanted was to know more about God. In a Sunday service, they asked who wanted to go to the Bible School in Maputo. I raised my hand. I would have to go to Maputo the next day. My mother looked at me surprised but I did not care. I had already decided to leave my job behind. I would go to Maputo with my son to study at the Bible School at Ministerio Arco Iris (Iris Global).

When I arrived at the centre, I realized that now everything was different. I dedicated myself to my studies and the baby stayed in the baby house. I finished the course in 2000, but I did not return to Gaza province because of the health problems my child had. There were many people who wanted to help me investigate the problem. Meanwhile, I began to cooperate with the pastors in evangelisation.

I became very involved in the work and I grew spiritually. Having salvation, I decided to end the relationship with the man who had four wives.

At this time, I already knew how to pray, and I sought God's will. My son fell very ill. I went to the hospital, but he did not get better. One day he and I took an HIV test at a clinic and the result was positive. There was no treatment. My son was hospitalised and died. This was the second child that I had lost. For me it seemed like the end of everything. I had lost two people I loved very much.

Soon after this, my mother fell ill and lost her life. Here I saw God sustaining me. Every morning I asked myself, "What will I do now?" But I felt that God was with me.

About my health, school and family

It was in 2001 that I became aware that I was HIV positive. There was no treatment, but I was checked at the hospital and began taking antiretovirals. During this period I had health problems. I was diagnosed with skin cancer, and I had tuberculosis. I followed the treatments and got better. At this time (2002), AIDS was synonymous with bad behaviour. It was very shameful to have this type of medical condition. Yet at the centre in Zimpeto there were people who supported me and prayed with me. Here I dreamed again, and I decided to go back to studying.

I said to myself that since I was in this situation I could not expect much and no one would want to marry me. I thought if I could not have children anymore I would study as a way to occupy myself.

I enrolled in 2002 to study grade 8, and from then on, I continued until completing grade 12.

With the support of Iris Ministries, I took a banking training course while preparing to go to University. I completed the course successfully.

In 2008, I took the entrance exam at two Universities but was not admitted to either. The following year, which was 2009, I only applied to one University and managed to get in. I dedicated myself to my studies and successfully completed my Bachelor's degree in Public Administration.

In my life I have had several difficult situations including illnesses and failed marriages. Yet all these situations have made me the person I am today. I am a mature woman firm on the rock that is JESUS. When I least expected that it was still possible to start a family after so much misfortune in my life, I met my husband.

I met this man when I had just arrived in Maputo. It was at a wedding where he was a friend of the groom and I was a friend of the bride. At that time he asked me to be his girlfriend and I told him straight away that it was impossible because I was sick. I told him about my health situation, but he said he still liked me. I said, "Here comes another one to fool me! Don't even think about it." He was studying and then went to work in a distant place, but whenever possible he would contact me to see if I was OK and to ask if I was married yet. During this period my biggest desire was to finish my degree and get married.

In 2011, we had a meeting and started talking about many things, including dating. This man's faith moved my heart. I began to pray for God to direct me. We started talking on the phone every day and then we started dating. With the help of God, and many people who loved us, we managed to get married in the same year and we now have a blessed family.

My husband Armando does not have HIV, and he supported me to continue taking medication. Two years after the wedding, we had the joy of becoming parents. Life smiled at me again and this time correctly without shame or embarrassment. I, who had lost everything, saw God restoring everything. By the grace of God, Armando and I now have two children:

Ebenezar and Emanuel. I have more than enough reasons to thank God because He is very good.

A few years ago I had the opportunity to go back to studying - this time to do an Academic Masters in Family and Community Therapy at the largest University in the country, Eduardo Mondlane University.

This course was so relevant to me. I acquired techniques that I needed to improve my way of behaviour and it was a complete package of everything that I needed to improve my work.

In 2014, I joined the team of workers at Iris Global in Zimpeto to work as a Secretary and shortly after I became the administrative assistant to the National Administrator. I am now Head of the Social Welfare and Reintegration Department within Iris Global.

This is an area that I love with all my heart. I love working with children and their families. I am working and at the same time fulfilling a dream. I love helping people. It is gratifying to realise that through our work several families are being reunited. For example, the joy I feel when I take a child off the street cannot be compared to anything. It is very gratifying.

My motto is: God is very good!

During this whole journey I feel that if it was not for God, maybe I would not be alive. If God has helped me this far it is because He has a purpose for me. I have learned to make myself available for God's will to be done in my life. On this journey, I've learned to wait on God.

The Bible passage Philippians 4:6-7 has sustained my faith:

> "Do not be anxious about anything, but in every situation, by prayer and petition, with thanksgiving, present your requests to God. And the peace of God, which transcends all understanding, will guard your hearts and your minds in Christ Jesus."

This passage taught me to pray, be grateful and trust God with my life.

Without a doubt today I can say with a clear voice that God was and has been kind to me. Where I am today was not through cleverness, but through the grace of God.

I have seen people who died of AIDS, cancer and tuberculosis, but I am here, alive and blessed, telling my testimony to the World.

This only happens when God is in control. My life is confirmation that God is merciful.

Ana Zaida at University graduation

Social welfare team -Ana Zaida, Hilda & Juliana

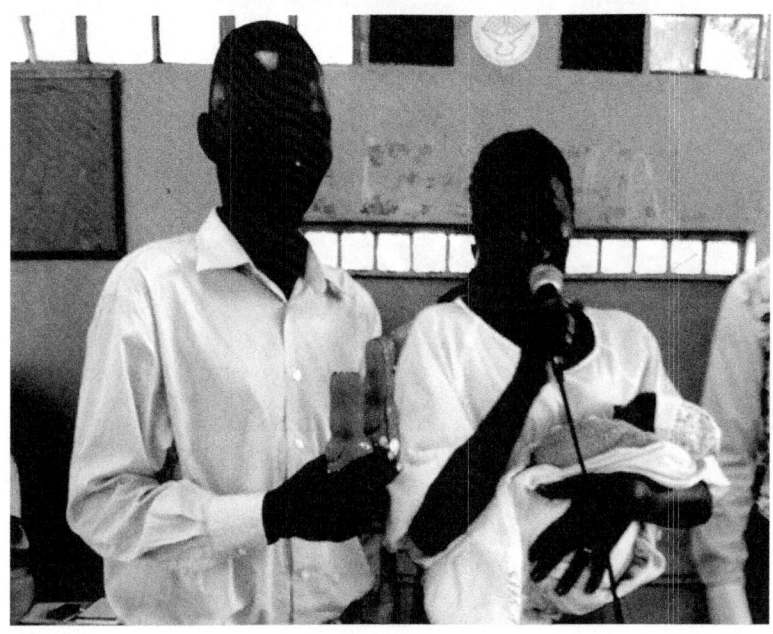
Ana Zaida and Armando

CHAPTER 3

Alimo Pedro

My name is Alimo Pedro, son of Ginove Chafrão Rhiyun and Luísa Pedro Herculano. I was born on 4 October 1996, in the province of Zambézia, district of Namacurra.

My father was a traditional healer and a polygamist, having several wives.

He had four children with my mother. My mother is Catholic. When my mother became pregnant with me, it took 5 months for her to be sure that she was carrying a foetus inside her. She went from healer to healer, and everyone said that she had something wrong with her and that they could not solve it. After many trips to the traditional healers in the fourth month, the last healer said that only the hospital could help them. So, she went to the hospital and had some tests done there. The nurse told my mother that she was pregnant. She was not convinced, and requested other tests over the following days. She was again confronted with the same news. I was born four months later.

As a baby, I was very sick, and I did not have the privilege of taking the first food that babies receive, because my mother did not have good breast milk. So, I had several illnesses, with swellings all over my body and sudden fainting spells. I went from traditional healer to traditional healer, with my parents in the hope of finding a solution. The problem continued, and the only solution given was to change "necklaces" (a traditional "charm" to be worn by babies) which my parents believed was "protection".

At 4 years old, I was still sickly. Our basis of survival was farming and depended on going to traditional healers. We all lived in a one-bedroom house sheltering four members. At that time, my mother had another baby after me. She was forced to leave me with my aunt and her sister. There I began to gain strength and gradually recovered, but I still wore the "necklace".

When I was five years old, my father lost his life, which was a great loss for my mother. At that time, I was living with my aunt. I was in good health. After a few months, my family (with counsel from the traditional healers) began to say that I was the chosen son to take over my father's work as a traditional healer. That is when the process of going from witch doctor to witch doctor began again, to gain experience.

In the days that followed, I was sent to the house of my father's assistant, so that he could become my mentor. I was now 6 years old. That same year, one of my uncles – my mother's brother - visited us. He lived in the capital of Mozambique, Maputo, and he told me that he wanted to take me there. This caused discord among my maternal and paternal families. After my father's death there was no longer any connection between the two sides, and they saw benefit in dividing the children. So, at dawn, I – together with my older brother and my uncle – left and came to Maputo.

When I arrived in Maputo in 2002, my older brother was ten years old. We enrolled at Khongolote Primary School. My uncle lived alone before we arrived and worked shifts. Everything here was new for my brother and me, but he had to become a man and take care of me in my uncle's absence.

You see, in a place you do not know, and being only ten years old, and taking care of a six-year-old, and sleeping in a house made of reeds with holes in it - fear easily takes over. In the mornings, when we were going to school, a neighbour's child would enter the house through the hole in the wall and steal some of the belongings.

We did not notice, because the missing things weren't ours. When my uncle came back from work, he would notice, call the two of us to explain, and of course we would say, "We didn't see anything." In fact, it was my brother who was questioned, and all the blame would fall on him. My uncle would beat him in a fierce way, right in front of me! I lived through that all year in 2002, and I still had the fainting problem.

My uncle would tie me up, like some petty thief, even though I was just a child. And whenever he did this, I would faint.

My brother ran away from home because he kept getting beaten up for things that my uncle said he did, and the neighbor kept coming through the hole and stealing. I felt alone on the nights when my uncle went to work: scared, fainting, and all alone.

I cried a lot. I longed to go back to my aunt's house: she had the patience to stay with me when I was sick, as a baby. Still, my brother would always come in the mornings to check on me and would run away well before my uncle returned. One morning, in 2003, my brother came as usual to see me, but we didn't expect our uncle to be nearby. As soon as he saw my brother coming in, he watched for a few minutes. When my brother was about to leave, my uncle appeared. My brother saw him and tried to escape but failed. What I saw next has affected me to this day. Of course, I forgave him: there is no resentment, but I wish I had not seen it!

My uncle tied my brother up so that he couldn't move. He beat him so badly that I thought I was going to lose him. My eyes were all red with tears. All day long, my uncle forbade me from giving him anything to eat, claiming that he was the one who was stealing from the house.

The next day, my uncle locked the door while I was inside with my brother. He told me not to go to school. When he left for work, I had no choice but to untie my brother. It would be one of the days when my uncle slept at work. So, that night, I ran away with my brother. We stayed at school overnight, in rooms where there was no security at all. My uncle came back from work and saw that we were not there. For a week we slept in the classrooms of that school, and I was very sick. During the day we had to go out and stay on the street!

Then one of the young people who knew my aunt said, "I know a place where you can get well." My brother, seeing how unhealthy I was, did not hesitate, and we went to Iris Ministries, where I received first aid and food!

I arrived at Iris Ministries in 2003, where I was welcomed. I met many children there. It seemed very strange to me, and I was very much alone. Little by little I started to open up. We arrived at the beginning of the year, where I was able to return to the first grade. The teacher, named Sandra, was very patient with me. She said, "I know you are smart, just try hard!"

I had a new routine: church on Tuesday, Thursday and Sunday, and dormitory small groups on Wednesdays, graduation services, and leisure activities. With all this, I started to feel like I was part of a family!

The first time I received presents for Children's Day (June 1) was a huge joy. I knew that I had to go to school, and I went believing I had a right to absolutely everything. When I was in second grade, with teacher Ivone, the words that my first-grade teacher had said began to come true. I became the best student in the class, thus winning the highest first grade prize offered by the school. This award brought many other awards.

When in 5th grade, I began to miss my parents. Although I was always the best in the class, I just won simple prizes on the podium – while other students only just passed the class, but their parents gave them bicycles and other games.

My whole family was left behind. No-one from my biological family was looking for me. Although I had a "new" family, and food, friends and toys, this emptiness continued to exist until 2009, when I met someone who was more present for me and understood my pain. With each positive response she motivated me. Her name was Clara, a missionary from Brazil.

What I really needed was someone who would be there for me full-time, who would understand me and let me cry on their lap! And missionary Clara was this person. I no longer saw her as a missionary. In her, I found a mother. It was at this time that I began to learn about my life and follow the teachings that I had been absorbing over the years, since being at Iris Ministries. Even though Zimpeto was a place of Christian worship, my mind was not yet capable of understanding the difference between the different religions. At that time, I just attended the programmes without any objection.

Clara was patient, and through her biblical teachings and reading programmes, we spent a lot of time together. She began to realise something was bothering me. I also wanted to open up to her, so I told her a lot of what I had experienced. She was moved, and she prayed for me. I immediately accepted Christ as Lord and Saviour, and from then, everything really moved forward. I began to feel full, without any emptiness, and Clara was always there by my side, as well as my friends and brothers.

I was baptised on 4 October 2010 - a significant day in my life.

At that time, I had the honour of leading a prayer group of students. One night we were at the house of prayer. We started at 6:00 pm for our usual programme (since on Fridays the siren for bedtime sounded at 9:00 pm). We began to seek God through our voices and lost track of time. I felt His presence and a very extraordinary touch. I felt that we were in another place.

When we stopped praying, it was almost 11:00 pm and there were some missionaries who had joined us, who were also praying. I was startled by the time, and thought, "What am I going to tell the dorm parents?", because there were girls there praying with me, and I was the leader there. It was forbidden to be there after the siren, and the girls had to stay in their area straight after dinner, but it was now 11:00 pm.

However, those who were there felt the presence of God and were grateful for the moment we had. It was one of the best experiences of God! From that day on, I had experiences with God, and I was invited to join the worship group in the prayer room. My journey as a preacher began at that time, and my mind was only on the Bible. Whenever someone looked for a Bible verse, most of the time they looked for me. In 2012, I participated in one of the biggest evangelical events, the Africa Mission, and shared the pulpit with great men of God. It was one of the most significant events that in my walk with God!

A Christian strives to abandon sin and asks Jesus for help to achieve this, every day following the narrow path that leads to God. Yes, it was not easy, and it is still not easy to deny my desires and follow the Creator's!

However, amid these choices I experienced several victories. I was the best student from 2nd to 10th grade. I felt that I brought pride and honour to the place where I grew up. This brought several consequences, including that girls were attracted to me. I remember that one time, one of the girls threw herself on top of me at school. I ran away from school and told Clara about this episode. We talked and prayed. I became a very thoughtful young man.

In all these experiences with God, something very strong prevailed in me. My goals were to unite my family into one, and for them to accept Christ. That was always boiling inside me. Everything else will come and go, except the Word of God!

After living the life of a "prince" in the centre, I ended up having a life outside the four walls of Iris Ministries. It was in January 2015 that I had to leave the centre where I grew up. Knowing about my walk with God, Papa Steve called me to talk. He encouraged me to move forward and said he had a house in Marracuene for me. This was at Iris Ministries' youth project - a centre with houses for older youth without family. I told him that I wanted to live with someone from my biological family so that I could get closer and get to know them, because since I separated from them in 2003, I had never seen them. The Reintegration/Social Welfare team had already located my uncle's house and informed him about my years in Iris Ministries.

Knowing this, Papa Steve did not stop me from going to live with my family. I went to my uncle's house: yes, the same house that my brother and I had fled from all those years ago due to mistreatment. This would be a great challenge.

When I arrived there, I was already attending the second year of the Analytical Chemistry course at the Industrial Institute in Maputo. In my uncle's house I was placed in the room where he kept dishes and pans, etc. In the first month, things went wonderfully. After that, when classes started, everything started to go wrong. The workload at the Institute was very heavy, from 7:30 am to 5:45 pm, and of course I arrived home very late. This annoyed my uncle, who said that this was not my home and that I had to make sure I got home on time. But lateness was unavoidable due to the time and means of transportation.

The second problem was with food. My uncle would cook for himself and wash the pots and pans. When 8 pm came, no matter how much I asked permission, the house would be locked. I was forced to sleep on the porch.

That made me think a lot. I had never had to sleep outside. Here, where there was family, there was no food, yet close by was a dormitory at Iris Ministries, where there was everything.

I swallowed it down, all alone, and then fell into depression. I ended up dropping out of the course in the second year. I stayed at home the entire year and was depressed. I heard my uncle's words day and night: "This house is not yours or your mother's." My mother was in Zambézia, about 1,600 Km away by road. I felt alone and trapped. That same year, I had the opportunity to travel to Zambézia. I remember telling Clara about the trip, and she did not take it well. I had to pretend to her that everything was fine with me. When I got there, the plan was to go and clean my father's grave and hold a ceremony in his memory. We were to ask our ancestors for luck and guidance. That is what my family believed in. When I heard about the plan, I refused to move and said to my mother. "Those who are alive don't care for me. Why should we seek the dead?" Then she said that her brother was right about everything he was doing. I felt like I was in a place that did not belong to me. They held the ceremony. My mother told her brother everything I had told her.

When I returned to Maputo, the first week I got sick. I was very down and out. I held on all year, but then I thought to myself: I know that I am smart and I know that if I lock myself in here I will have nothing. Let me get up again.

It was in 2016 that I gained strength and returned to study at the Industrial and Commercial Institute of Matola. I started studying and tutoring and I remember that at that time. Papa Steve spoke to me at his house saying, "You can talk to me directly about anything related to school." He gave me a monthly amount to cover the basic needs of the training. It is important to note that I had already been receiving this amount since I left the ministry. But at home, this time was no different to before. I would leave the Institute, go to tutor, and then come home late. I would even have to sleep in the bathroom, which - being outside – well, you can imagine. Mosquitoes, cockroaches and the cold would overwhelm me, and I would only be able to go inside at 3 am when my uncle would go to the bathroom. He would say, "Do you want to scare me to death? Why are you sleeping in my bathroom?"

I would just cry. I was very thin and hungry. Sometimes I would run out of transport money because I needed to use the money for food. I would then leave Matola at 7am on foot and would be late for lessons.

Praise God, my performance at the Institute was always positive. I passed the second year in 2017. At the beginning of the year, I saw a beautiful young woman there. Just seeing her made me feel bashful. However, I never spoke to her because I knew about my situation - I rarely had a bed to sleep in. I became friends with her and whenever I went to school, I liked to talk to her. She understood me and listened to me, or so I thought. I started to get used to sleeping in the bathroom, sleeping in the fog, sleeping without dinner. I became familiar with almost everything I suffered alone in that backyard. I was happy at school and at Iris Ministries when I gave lessons because I like to help others.

In 2017, I came down with a hidden case of malaria. I remember that I got sick going to the Institute every day. I preferred to go there sick than stay in that house. It happened to be at the end of the month when I got my salary from my tutoring, and so I went to the health centre in Matola. I had a blood test, and it was found that the malaria was in an advanced stage. The doctor said if I had gone a few more days without taking medication, I could have died. My haemoglobin was low. I took the prescription and showed it to Clara. Her eyes were red. I believe she felt that something was going badly for me at home, but I didn't tell her anything.

However, even with this illness, there was no peace at home. That same year, my uncle fell ill and was at the Central Hospital in Maputo. I left my studies early every day, skipping classes, to prepare food for him and take it to the hospital. Even so, this did not soften my uncle's heart.

In 2018, already in the third year and with less time pressure, I would get home early from the Institute and spend more time at home. When I started spending more time there, another topic started. "You only eat, and you bring nothing here. It's not your house or your mother's," my uncle would say.

At that time, I would buy onions and soup here and there. After hearing my uncle's complaints, I started buying boxes of dried fish. One day in December 2018, I bought the fish, put them in the freezer, and went to spend a weekend at a cousin's house in Matola. When I came back from my cousin's house, my uncle was sitting there waiting for me and said, "You bought fish and put them in my freezer and you didn't buy any electricity. Do you want to waste my energy?"

He had turned off the freezer and everything was rotten. To be honest, I felt like throwing the freezer at him, but I kept crying and saying to myself, "What have I done to my family?" I cleaned the freezer and stayed. Every morning, I would get up in the middle of a very tense atmosphere, and hope that it would soon be time to go to the Institute, but unfortunately or fortunately, my classes eventually came to an end. I passed, and all that was left was an internship.

I went home and told my uncle: "I finished and passed everything. All I need is an internship." My uncle responded, "I'm not looking for internships for criminals."

In 2019, I would leave the house early to go to an internship, and come back late, without eating anything - and even then, I had to sleep in the bathroom or on the porch. If there was no rain to get me wet, there was heat and mosquitoes to attack me. That situation made me angry, and I no longer had my studies to relieve me. I left my uncle's house for two months and stayed with friends. By that time, I had already found an internship in "Aguas de Mozambique" in the city.

When I had been at a friend's house for more than two months, I went back to my uncle's house. I could not stand having to go through everything I was going through. I called Clara and said, "I need to talk to you." She immediately said, "Alimo, I'll be waiting for you tomorrow."

The next day, I went to see her. We sat down and I told her everything that I have written here. She cried and said, "We'll fix it this week." Clara regretted that I had not told her everything before.

It did not take long for an Iris house to be available for me to stay in. A few days later, I moved into the new house!

This change made my family angry. My mother called me and said, "You abandoned the person who paid for your first-class schooling, the person who took care of you, the person who gave you a roof over your head."

In January 2020, job opportunities opened. The company where I had an internship hired me. In the same year, I was admitted to Eduardo Mondlane University. I did not hide my emotions. I shared them with the people who were happy with me: Clara and her husband Augusto, Papa Steve and Mana Ros, and others.

The joy did not stop there. As a gift, I received a piece of land from Papa Steve and Mana Ros. My heart could not handle the emotions anymore.

One Saturday, I was surprised by a visit from my cousins, uncles, aunts, and sisters-in-law. I welcomed them. I had no idea that they knew where I was. I welcomed them and took the opportunity to tell them about the great achievements in my life. It seemed a joke to them. One of my cousins said "Why are you happy and why do you keep studying? In 2027 you will die."

When my family left, I prayed there in the entrance to the room. I told my spiritual mentor Clara, and we prayed. It is very good to have a spiritual mentor. It was not long before my mother called to say, "Your luck is due to your father and your grandfather - who is the father of that uncle of yours that you abandoned. Now that you have a job, do you think you won't need him?"

I replied, "Mum, for many years I was talked about and treated badly by him. Even after finding a job, my uncle still threw stones at me." However, I became more and more mature and strong.

In the same year, 2020, I met the young woman I mentioned before, and the relationship grew. I introduced her to Clara and her husband Augusto. In 2021, I became the boyfriend of this beautiful and wonderful young woman, who was part of my therapy, just because of the attention she gave me. She became very important in my life.

In 2022, my uncle got sick again and needed blood. In fact, he called me while I was asleep. The next day, I returned the call without success. I sent a message and there was no response. I did not know what was happening. Only later did I hear from one of my aunts that the uncle had gathered the family in the province and said, "Alimo said he would never come to my house, and I prefer him to die without me." When I found out about that, I talked to my fiancée, and she calmed me down.

At one of the family gatherings at my uncle's house, I asked to speak, and I told him everything I had been through. I challenged him about everything he, my uncle, had been making up in the family. The idea was not to embarrass him. It was really to leave everything clean and not to hear any more rumours and accusations. When I had finished, the family said nothing, including him. From that day on, he started to respect me. He would call me and come to visit. I went to his house without any problems.

In December 2023, my uncle lost his life while I was away on a work trip. They waited for me to return, and I then took care of all the funeral protocol. One day, after the whole thing was over, I was walking with my mother and some neighbours stopped me and said, "You are different. After everything your uncle put you through, you still visited him and buried him. Congratulations." When we got home, my mother asked me to stay a little while and started talking about how her brother had apologized for everything he put me through, and for everything he did to us back in 2003. I told her that my heart is clean.

Today, I am a young man who helps other young people, and takes care of his family. Together with my fiancée, we are writing a new story. We are young people who fear God. I often speak about Jesus to my biological mother. I emphasize this "biological" part because I have two women who fill the place of a mother in my life. I am blessed professionally and in all aspects of my life.

Thank God, I have a beautiful and loving partner by my side, to whom I will soon get married. Trust only in God! Wait on Him!

Alimo at work

Alimo with fianceé Leicha

CHAPTER 4

Aniceta Martins

MY NAME IS Aniceta Martins. I was born on 15 February 2001. I grew up in a family with six sisters. Four of us were from my own father. I was the youngest, and my Mum had two more daughters with other partners.

When I was six years old, I already had an idea of what was going on around me. At that time, my parents' relationship was not going well and they ended up separating. That is where lots of problems began.

My father drank a lot and smoked a lot. Living in the house with my Dad was scary and dangerous. He sexually abused my sisters. But at the time, I did not know that, until the day he tried to have sex with me. I refused. Since then, I was never my father's favourite. He ignored me. Everything was for my sisters, and that was because he made them his wives.

Consequently, my Dad was sick. He had HIV/AIDS and transmitted the disease to my sisters. At that time, in 2008, I lost one of my sisters. So I went to live with my mother, and for the same reason, HIV/AIDS, I ended up losing her in 2010. I was nine at the time. I had to go back to live with my father. When I went back there, everyone was already sick: my two sisters and my father. At that time, I had to learn to take care of them. This included washing, cooking, and preparing everything for them, not to mention having to look for food. This was a very difficult situation.

In 2012, I lost another sister, but my father never changed. He only increased his addictions. At that time, one of my younger sisters from another father had to come to live with us, because she also lost her father. This sister from another father was very sick, as was my father, because he kept making her his wife. We didn't know Jesus. No one went to church. It was as if all that mattered was trying to live.

My biggest task was to protect my younger sister and myself, so that we would not run the same risk of becoming my father's wives. Living in fear - caused by the person who was supposed to be our protector - was too disturbing. I felt constant anger and resentment towards him. I looked at him as an aberration because everything that happened in my life; every loss we endured was his fault. No one could tell me otherwise, because I was the one who experienced every misfortune we went through.

I remember in detail the days when we slept without eating and the days when I had to knock on the neighbours' doors to ask for some food for my father. My sister and my father needed medication as they were no longer in a condition to do anything for themselves.

One day a miracle occurred. I will never forget that day when the Social Welfare team from Iris Ministries put hope in my eyes, promising to take care of me and my sisters. As I said at the time, we didn't know Jesus. But hope arose. It quickly became apparent that I really needed Jesus to change the situation I was in. I really wanted Jesus to change my story, and that day was when it happened.

The Social Welfare team from Iris Ministries people said that it was possible for my life to change. It was as if I were dreaming. Then my sisters and I went to live at the center in Zimpeto. They welcomed children like my sisters and me: children who needed hope, affection, care, lots of love, and lots of Jesus.

I lost my father that year, 2014, as he was very sick. The people at the centre tried to take very good care of my sister Benedita, giving her all their love and care, so that she could recover. But the disease had already taken over her body, and she could not fight the sickness anymore. I lost her too, and it was very sad. My story is a tale of loss.

I continued to live at the center for a long time, together with my younger sister. We learned and experienced many things, including meeting Jesus and receiving him as our Lord and Saviour. I realized that thanks to Him I did not have to suffer anymore. Thanks to Him, my sister and I had life. Thanks to His mercy there were people like those from Iris Ministries with huge hearts and empathy to support us and show us how to move forward; show us how strong and capable we were of achieving great things.

We had a great school and a good education. That was essential. We studied hard, and freed ourselves a little from our past suffering. In 2019, my sister went to live with my aunt - who claimed not to know me and literally rejected me.

In 2020, I was reintegrated into a local family.

When I finished my 12th grade, I gained entrance to university, thanks be to God and the unconditional help of Iris Ministries. Then, in 2022, I lost my younger sister, because she was found dead, and it was very painful.

In 2023, I moved to live with another family because the relationship with the first family was difficult. I went to live with a wonderful family from the church (Laurinda, the widow of Pastor Nico and their 5 children). I gained a mother and siblings and it had a huge impact on my life.

Today, I am 23 years old. I am finishing my university degree in Accounting and Auditing with the help of Iris Ministries, Papa Steve and Mana Ros, and their friends with kind hearts who help with the necessary finances to pay for my university fees. I feel very supported and covered in prayer.

Therefore, I have so much to thank God for. My words and my soft heart seem too little to thank God for the huge difference He has made in my life. I have achieved so much and have peace in my heart every day.

Today, when I look back, I have survived because the Lord helped me. I can only thank Him for the price He has paid, and continues to pay for my sake, so that I may have life and abundance; so that I may be surrounded by people with big hearts and humility. The Lord gave me so much strength and changed my story. He made me believe in the impossible.

Aniceta

Stories of Hope

With housemates Anifa & Fatima

With Pastor Laurinda

CHAPTER 5

Armando Nguenha

MY NAME IS Armando Fenias Nguenha. I was born in the city of Maputo on 27 December 1992. I was my parents' first child. My paternal grandmother tells me that after I was born, my parents were warned by the Hospital that I had a type of visual impairment, and that sooner or later I would go blind. She also maintains that my parents ignored this warning. Certainly, my eyesight deteriorated by the age of three or four. At that point, out of nowhere, I started seeing darkness. My aunts said that my eyes changed colour, and I could no longer go anywhere in the house alone without support.

Parents and siblings

My father was born in the Marracuene District and migrated to the city of Maputo with his parents and siblings to the Chamanculo neighbourhood, where he grew up until he met my mother. She was also born in the Chamanculo neighbourhood. However, she grew up in Tenga in the rural District of Moamba, in the province of Maputo. Due to the intensification of the years of civil war that had spread in the interior of the province of Maputo, my mother's family was forced to return to Chamanculo (where my maternal grandfather had two residences).

Unfortunately, his decision caused my mother to leave school, because in the city, life was expensive, and different from the rural district where they had depended on the farm. Therefore, she was forced to look for work. She met my father whilst working as a maid in a house that was no more than 900m from his parents' house: they were almost neighbours and travelled the same route when going to work. They began to date, and then she got pregnant with me. She had to live with my father in his parents' house.

Because I was born with visual impairment, even though it did not manifest itself at the beginning, there began to be a barrage of accusations. In Africa it is very common to blame disability (whether at birth or acquired) and other abnormal happenings on witchcraft. This happened in my family, with both sides constantly accusing each other. My mother's family accused my paternal grandmother of having given some medicine to my mother while she was breastfeeding. On the other hand, my paternal grandmother accused my mother of negligence. There were other family members who went even deeper, saying that it was something hereditary, as my maternal grandfather's mother was blind.

This whole climate caused some discomfort in my parents' relationship. It was said that I was not my father's son, a situation that was worsened by the fact that my father drank a lot of alcohol and was a womaniser, as well as being the son of a polygamist. He impregnated another woman, who was also forced to come and live with him in his parents' house, with their child – my first brother. His mother was perfect in my grandmothers' eyes, but my father continued to seek my mother. Their relationship was volatile at this time with a lot of fighting. Consequently, I was moved from house to house, sometimes living with my maternal grandmother, or at the house of uncles or aunts.

During one of my mother's returns to my father's house, she ended up getting pregnant and had a girl. This was the second child on my father's side - and the first on my mother's side - to be born without a disability, which made the relationship between the two families reasonable. It seemed like my parents could stay together forever, but that did not happen, because my father got the mother of my brother pregnant again. She had another boy, and this generated a very ugly fight with my mother, who did not want this woman and her sons around. She definitively ended the relationship with my father, but he insisted on maintaining it, which forced my mother into a decision that completely changed my life.

She left the city, returned to Tenga, joined a group of friends, and decided to emigrate to neighbouring South Africa. She wanted to find a job and to distance herself even further from my father. This was in 1997, when I was 5 years old and was still in the process of receiving treatment for my eyes.

She says that she wanted to emigrate with me and my sister, but my grandfather did not let her, because we would do it illegally: entering through the bush, crossing the fence and not through the official border. It would be very risky because there were people who went and never came back. So, she ran away while I was with my grandparents on the farm, taking my sister who was only one year old at the time. She met another man and had four more children, so I have five siblings born to my mother and two to my father.

Disability history and education

As I have already mentioned above, my vision deteriorated between the ages of three and four. At this point my family took me to the central hospital in Maputo, where I underwent surgery on my right eye. They recommended that I should continue with treatment and later have an operation on the second eye. After my mother fled to South Africa, my father became an alcoholic as it was believed that she had died in the bush, and no one knew her whereabouts. This affected his capacity to provide me with assistance and, in 2001, my father died, which made the situation even more complicated.

From that moment on, I was under the sole responsibility of my elderly grandmother, who only lived off the farm and the little support that my uncles gave her. I still had no news of my mother and so I felt like an orphan.

It was one of these days, when I was going to have my eyes checked, that my aunt, who was also accompanying my cousin, saw a missionary from Iris Ministries who had a child with her. They had a conversation where the missionary offered my aunt the opportunity to take my cousin to the centre for some support. My grandmother was grateful, but preferred that *I* should get the help, so she took the missionary to me and introduced my grandmother and another aunt who was with her. They told my story and said that they were having difficulty buying medicines and continuing with the treatment; that there was an operation that was postponed due to lack of resources. The missionary sympathised with the situation and ended up giving me the address of the centre and the necessary requirements for me to live there.

My grandmother was anxious about this because she feared losing someone else: what she wanted was simply financial support so that I could continue with the treatments. However, my aunts felt I would be better cared for elsewhere. There had been an incident where I got lost while playing with my cousins and was eventually retrieved from the police station. Another time, I got lost and was then found by my father's friend. So, in order to keep me safe, my grandmother had to take me with her wherever she went, which was already risky due to her age, as it was difficult to get around on the busy roads of Maputo.

After convincing my grandmother to accept that I be admitted to the children's centre, my aunt and my grandmother approached the centre, and explained my situation. After presenting the documents required by the management, I was welcomed and started living there.

It was not easy at first, as it was a great challenge having to live with children I did not know, especially with very reduced vision. Over time, I ended up socialising, as I made many friends and some of them helped me with whatever was necessary. My grandmother came to see me at least once a week, and sometimes I went to visit her.

I continued with treatment, under the assistance of the centre but, according to one of the doctors, it was already too late to go ahead with the operation. The doctor recommended that I go to the Institute for the Visually Impaired in Beira, so I could study. It is worth mentioning that, up to that time, I had not been enrolled in school. When I started living in Iris Ministries I went to classes, but I could not read or write. I only listened.

In 2003, I travelled to Beira with another girl, also visually impaired, whose father worked at the centre. But before that, while we were preparing for this trip, I went to visit my grandmother so I could say goodbye to her. That was when my mother reappeared: a warm afternoon on 23 December 2002, right when we were preparing to return to the city. It was a reunion with a mixture of feelings: anger, joy, sadness, etc., because at the time I did not understand much, and I had in mind that my mother had abandoned me and had ended up in the bush, swallowed by a lion. She apologized for what had happened but said she had already found another husband and that she had now come to get me, so I could live with them. My grandmother and I preferred that I go to Beira to study, although my grandmother was still anxious about this, because the conditions of the journey would be dangerous. After Christmas, I returned to Zimpeto, along with my grandmother and mother. Some aunties from the dormitory explained to my mother the importance of me going to Beira. She accepted this, and with sadness, ended up letting me go.

When I arrived in Beira, the longest trip I have ever made, I stayed at the house of a missionary, who shortly afterwards enrolled me at the Institute for the Visually Impaired. I started in the preparatory class learning Braille graphics, a system that blind people use to read and write, using touch and some technological equipment.

Here, I had one of the most difficult challenges because, when I left Maputo, I imagined that I would live in the house of the missionary who welcomed us, but that was not true. I was admitted to the student home that the school offers to students who come from places far from the city of Beira. There, I joined other people with visual impairments, which was a very good experience, as there were people of almost all ages. Many of the visually impaired students could walk throughout the city without needing a sighted guide, and they carried out their activities independently. Yet, our lifestyle was challenging: there were food problems, the security was not good as the older boys beat and robbed the younger ones, and the layout of the buildings meant we had to cross roads. I will say more about this shortly.

We complained to the missionary, and the following year we stayed for a while with her, but due to the increased fuel needs (her house was 30km from the school) she convinced us to go back to living at the school. Luckily, I had become smart and knew how to defend myself, and my desire to study made me ignore poor nutrition and the other difficulties that existed, and just focus on my objectives. Unfortunately, my colleague couldn't stand it and chose to return home, which I did not understand at the time.

The following year, the school transitioned to become the new IDV (Beira Institute for Visual Disabilities). Management was taken over by priests, under the umbrella of Portuguese assistance, and everything was improved: the food, the conditions of the dormitories, and security, were among additional aspects that the old home did not offer.

The old home had been divided into three buildings. First was the school, where the administrative block was located, along with classrooms, kitchen, cafeteria, a courtyard, and a field where we played sports. Then, on the other side of the road, there was the women's home where the girls would sleep, as well as some younger boys so they could have assistance from the guards. Third, about 100m beyond that, was the men's home.

The new facilities were all in a single building. There was an administrative block, with classrooms, all connected by a corridor. In the middle was a courtyard and a garden that separated the bedrooms, the cafeteria, and other departments, making the building accessible and practical. Children did not have to cross roads all the time (except for those students who were already in high school, as the school taught only up to seventh grade).

I ended up building a good reputation because, despite my limitations, I was able to travel around the city. We took part in a children's programme on radio Mozambique. We played soccer for the blind, and athletics. We went to the House of Culture, where I learned to play the piano, and we liked to go to the beach, which was less than two kilometres from IDV. Within the home, I was part of cultural groups, taking part in theatre, choral singing and dance group - activities that contributed a lot to my personal development, because I learned to be interactive, competitive and social.

It should be noted that IDV is a complete primary special school designed to teach students with visual impairments and, after primary education, the students are integrated into regular schools to continue their studies. Therefore, in 2010 I finished my seventh grade and enrolled at Secondary school, where my other challenges began. I was used to being in a classroom with colleagues in the same condition as me, all users of Braille. I was used to teachers being prepared in how to deal with students with special needs and delivering special classes with a focus on visual impairment. Now, I started studying in a class where I was the only student with a visual impairment. I often came across teachers who did not know how to deal with my situation, a situation that continued until higher education. But, through my experiences of primary education and of learning from other students who had already gone through this experience, and with the help of sighted colleagues, I managed to face the challenge.

My colleagues read out what was on the board, and dictated notes, as well as reading questions on test days. There were also sensitive teachers who came to talk to me, and together we found solutions on how I could feel included in the classroom, such as: not just writing on the board but dictating the notes, dictating what I wrote, anticipating the questions of the assessments so that I could transcribe them in Braille or then approach the IDV for printing in Braille, or translating the test written in Braille into regular handwriting for the teacher to mark. All of this forced me to work harder to be able to overcome these difficulties, and to make people believe that disability does not prevent us from studying.

In 2012, a project appeared within IDV that gave us the opportunity to learn how to use smartphones in an accessible way, using screen readers for the IOS system as well as Windows. We explored the NVDA (Non Visual desktop Access), a screen reader, which allowed more autonomy in how we dealt with technology. Some colleagues could afford smartphones, and were now able to use them without depending on a third person to read messages or perform any operations. I progressed until I was able to use the Windows system (through NVDA), from mastering Word to browsing the web, which greatly facilitated my preparation and participation in schoolwork. The institution had some computers we could use. A few years later, the director of Iris Zimpeto offered me my first computer, with which I could do my schoolwork independently.

In 2014, with the support of Iris Zimpeto, I attended the Language Institute with the opportunity to participate in a trip to Zimbabwe to learn intensive English. This was an extraordinary experience, as I was able to show that it is possible to learn even in the context of being the only person with a disability in a specific group.

In 2015, I finished general education and had to be reunited with my family, which was not easy. I did not know who I would live with because my grandmother, who had always welcomed me, had already died, eight years before that. There was only one uncle who could receive me, but his house did not have enough space. It was at this point that the Zimpeto centre offered to build a room in this uncle's house, and he was then willing to welcome me, which was a blessing for me and the family in general.

After finishing general education, there was confusion about where I would continue my studies. My dream was to study outside the country and to do something related to Technology or International Relations. My situation was new for everyone: IDV had organised the transition from primary to secondary education; Iris Zimpeto had helped with school uniforms and transport to and from Maputo at the end of term; yet there was no clear plan or precedent for the next step of my education.

The Zimpeto centre agreed to support me with Higher Education costs, and I enrolled at The Eduardo Mondlane University in Maputo to study Education Organisation and Management. I continued to live with my uncle during university, but there were tensions. My uncle thought my time there would only be temporary and there was not a good atmosphere with my cousins. I talked about this with the leaders of the Zimpeto centre, and they built a house for me on my grandmother's land. For me, this was another great achievement, because - without the support of the Zimpeto base - I do not know what my life would be like. In my family there are very few young people with higher education and their own housing.

In 2023, I graduated with great enthusiasm, celebrated by friends and family, as well as by the Directors of Zimpeto.

My conversion

I was born into a religious family. My grandparents were leaders in the Mazione church (a religious sect - an offshoot of Christianity involving many rituals). My uncle is still the leader of a church he created.

When I started living in the Zimpeto centre, I continued to go to church because the centre had a congregation there and our way of life was guided by the Bible. Similarly, when I arrived in Beira, I lived with a missionary: yet even so, I never had any personal experience of Christ. When I lived at IDV, there were people from all over the country with different cultures, religions and beliefs, which made me question what I believed. I tried out different church congregations and I ended up identifying a lot with one called Centro de Peniel Adoracão. Then, at the end of 2010, a couple from a ministry called Young Life came to IDV and talked with us, sharing verses from the Bible. The following year, I decided to go to a vigil programme they led for boys at the house of a friend. It was a very fun night, as it was a relaxed way of preaching the gospel: there were lots of games, music, and stimulating conversations.

After that, I started to participate in their Biblical studies, where I strengthened my understanding about Jesus. Shortly afterwards, Young Life organized a very dynamic camp in one of the tourist areas in Beira. The theme of the camp was "You will know the truth, and the truth will set you free" (John 8:32). It was here that I had the opportunity to have an encounter with Christ. I also had an opportunity to forgive my mother: the previous year, she had explained why she had abandoned me but, even so, I remained hurt. However, after deciding to forgive her, I was free and began to be a much happier person than before.

Currently, I have been blessed to be able to help people who, for some reason or another, think of giving up on life or choose bad paths. I have presented Christ as a solution to these people, an activity that I do in collaboration with Young Life. This has given me the opportunity to make friends and influence people.

I currently advocate for the rights of people with disabilities, particularly young people, an activity that I do voluntarily, together with FAMOD (Forum of Mozambican Organisations for People with Disabilities).

At this moment, I am here, writing my story to the world, to show that disability is not the end but the beginning of something to be discovered. Disability does not stop us from dreaming. What we must do is overcome mental laziness, have faith in God and search for solutions to resolve or overcome the barriers we are facing.

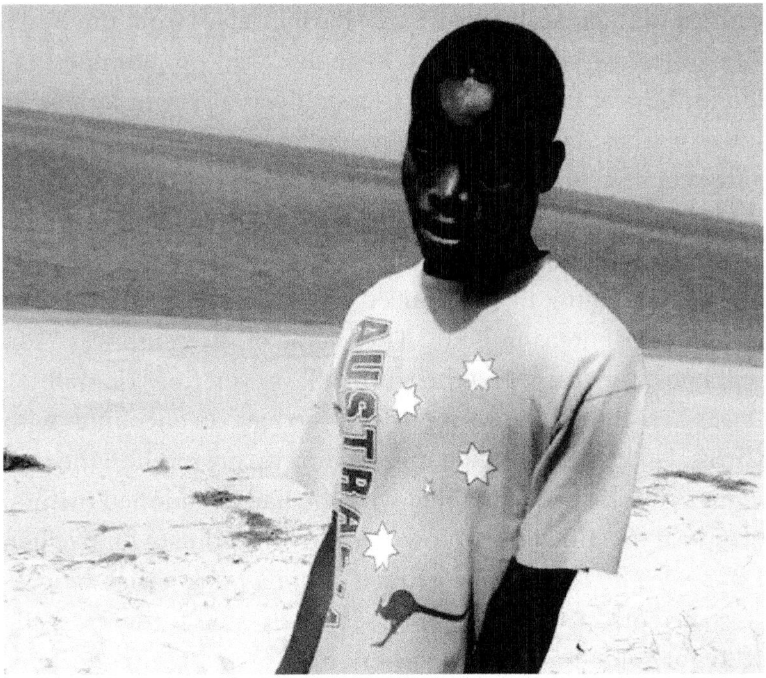

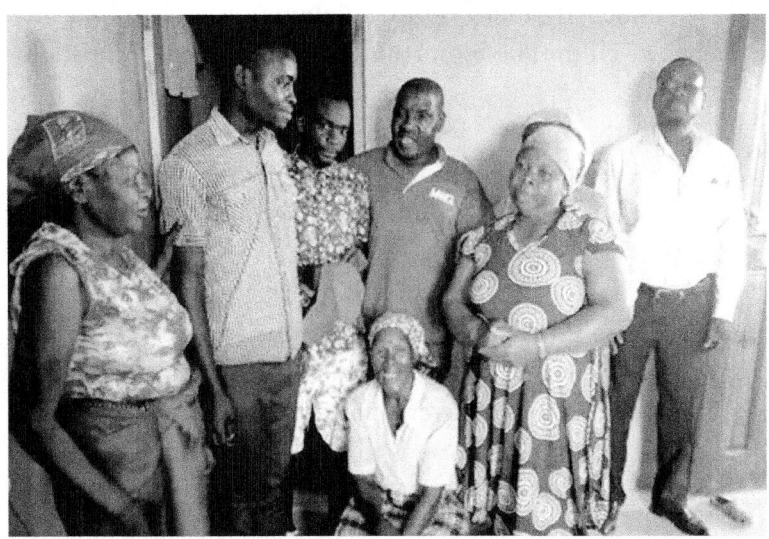

Armando as a youth

Armando with his family

University graduation

CHAPTER 6

Araújo Mapanzene

My name is Araújo Mapanzene. I am 35 years old, and I was born in Maputo, Mozambique. I grew up in a very poor family.

My brother and I used to go to school, and my mother always told us to study hard, because this can guarantee a good future for you.

In March 2003, I was visiting my uncle for the school holidays. One morning, I was with my cousin, when my father came and told us, "Mother has died." We thought that the person who had died was *his* mother, and we were not very worried at first. Then, I asked again, "Whose mother has died?" He replied, "*Your* mother." I was very sad that day.

After my mother's death, we stayed with our father, who used to travel for his job. One day, my father went away forever. We were three children without any knowledge of life. We were all alone, without anything to eat. We stopped going to school and were living by the generosity of others.

Our aunt (my mother's sister) collected us to live with her

in her house. We went back to school, but life was not good because she did not have enough to support us and her own child. Once again, we stopped school. This time, our lives were going to be ruined, and there was no future for us.

I do not know how my aunt knew about Iris Ministries, but she started working on documentation to register us there. It was not easy to register us, but after a long time she succeeded, and we were accepted to live at Zimpeto.

The first days were not easy for us because we met many different people with unfamiliar and new behaviour. I confess it was a hard time for us, and sometimes I thought about running away, but I realised there was no other place to go. I started to go to church and learn more about God.

I started to go to school and I enjoyed it. I realised the benefits of being on the base, with education, care, food and safety.

There was no High School at this time at Iris Ministries, so I went to a Catholic school outside the base. It was good for me because I met many friends. I was on the Honour board at the school as the best student. I loved talking to other students about common interests in Maths and Science.

Meanwhile, at Zimpeto, I met Arthur Connor, a visitor from Australia who taught Mathematics to students who wanted extra help. This was very good because I learned a lot with him. He taught me some methods to solve Maths problems that we do not use here in Mozambique.

Following this, I gained entry to the Industrial Institute, and then to a prestigious university - "University Eduardo Mondlane" - to study Chemistry.

One day, a former teacher of mine called me and asked, "Are you working?" I said, "No, I am continuing my studies at university." Then, she told me there was a company that was recruiting for engineering students, who might have an interest in mining, to register for an internship. So, I registered myself.

The company (Shlumbergeer) called us for two aptitude tests. I succeeded and went on to the next stage, which included an interview. Only two people who studied Chemistry were called for the interview. The interview was in the best hotel in Maputo and it was the first time I had been inside a hotel. We had two full days of interviews plus one more day for me to do Chemistry tests.

Soon after, I was in the computer room at Iris Ministries, checking my email. I received an email to say that I had succeeded in the interview and that I should prepare a passport and other documents to travel to South Africa for English classes.

I printed the offer letter and showed it to Papa Steve. I was very happy and the salary that the company was offering was very good for me. It would be the first time that I had received a salary.

I asked Papa Steve for the money for the passport and other documents. After I got my passport, I sent a copy to the company. Shlumbergeer sent me airline tickets. I had been thinking that I would go by bus to South Africa. This was my first flight and my first journey out of Maputo in my whole life.

I travelled to South Africa for English school and a medical checkup. I underwent many medical examinations, but everything went well. I passed the English school and the medical checkup. I had been worried about this because I was not sure that my health was 100%.

Having passed everything, it was now time to go to work. I was sent to Tanzania, for my first job with the company, and after that I had many job opportunities all around the world. Thanks be to God for everything He is doing in my life.

I have done a lot of good things in my life. I have a beautiful family, despite losing my son last year in a terrible accident. My morale and my strength were taken from me after this loss, and

I am now seeing a very good psychologist. No father deserves to see his son die. We always pray to see our children grow up with good health. I think that is a motivation to work hard.

God is giving me good things, and I am able to help people that do not have many things.

I read somewhere: "Always do good to everyone and never do harm to anyone." My dream is to open a centre that helps people and to give them opportunities. Despite our past, the future is bright and there are opportunities (with help) to succeed in life.

I have now bought some land for my future project. I know God is faithful.

Papa Steve and Araújo

Araújo at work

Araújo and his wife Mércia

CHAPTER 7

Beatriz Timane

My name is Beatriz José Timane and I was born on 29 November 1985.

In my childhood I lived with my father and mother, but our living conditions were extremely poor. We lived a very difficult life in terms of food, clothing and schooling.

Our house was made of caniço (bamboo) and we all lived in one room. At times, snakes would come in and we had to sleep in that room with the snakes.

My father and my mother did not have work. At times, my father did odd jobs, but my mother was mute and was not able to do anything. She often took me to a neighborhood called Gazene in the district of Marracuene. I began looking for opportunities to be self-sufficient.

When my mother died, I had health problems. There were marks almost everywhere on my head, and on my face. My knees were red raw, and my welts were ready to burst. I felt that perhaps I was close to death!

Thanks be to God, Mama Aida and Papa Rolland came to

Mozambique and saved my life. They took me urgently to the house they rented in Maputo City. When I got there, Mama Aida could not even bathe me because my condition was critical. She took me to Maputo Central Hospital where I was hospitalised and had medical assistance.

Every day, I received prayers from Mama Aida and others who accompanied her. I was covered with bandages from head to toe. I had to have plastic surgery. I was discharged and started living in the Iris base in Chihango. My arrival was seen as miraculous because no-one had expected to see me again. While I was there, Mama Aida always checked on my health.

Then we all moved to Boa Nova in Machava. We had very few pans and little food to cook with. I remember living on fresh milk and popcorn for a week.

During my free time, I liked to play with other children, study at the Bible School, go to school (basic education) and to learn anything. I also liked to teach other children Bible stories. There was a church dance group, and I was involved a lot in the theatre and dramas.

After the Boa Nova Centre, we moved to the new Iris base in Machava. We started by sleeping in tents, then in a caniço house, and, eventually, little by little, we built a block house. We suffered from a great lack of water. It was normal to bathe ten children in one 20-litre bath!

There was a huge flood tragedy in 2000, when all the houses in Machava sunk under water, and we lost a lot of things. We were flooded almost up to our necks. We had to start on new land at Zimpeto.

Thank God, we could go there. That is where we had First Aid and healthcare in the middle of the floods. When the Iris base at Zimpeto was first established, we stayed in tents and caniço huts and then we moved to block dormitories. We always prayed and fasted for everything to go well within the centre.

I had a vision from God, who showed me to start to study with the help of Iris Global. I suffered and struggled with my studies. At nine years old, I did not read or write. I did not stop studying. I almost gave up, but with the help of God, and people who encouraged me, I kept going.

During my early years at Zimpeto, I had an educator named Delfina, and a schoolteacher named Sandra. Their role was fundamentally to teach, to educate, and to look after my health and spiritual well-being. They were very patient with me and the other children. My teacher, Sandra, really loved and cared for me. (Later, when I completed my degree in Human Resources, I invited Sandra to be my "Graduation Godmother".)

As time went on, I continued my studies while crying in my heart. I continued to have problems with many things and understanding most subjects. It was difficult for friends to help me with my schoolwork. I continued to do work based on the examples the teacher did on the board. By my strength and determination, I continued to study until I finished 12th grade.

I left the Iris base when I was 18 years old. My life situation started to become difficult again because I went to my family home. Almost none of my family went to church and they lived a life without understanding and without love between them.

I got married, and then I suffered because of my mother-in-law. She always spoke to me without respect, and sometimes she wanted me to leave home. The family did not care about me. I persisted because people advised me to stay with my husband. We bought a house with the help of Iris Global. My husband started to mistreat me psychologically and physically: sometimes he hit me. He started not paying attention to me or my children, Augusto and Christalina. He often drank alcohol. Every time he rejected me, I went to Iris Global for help with health, food and other school expenses.

I entered University, but things continued to be difficult. It was a critical situation that even today is difficult to forget. It took all my courage and strength to survive. I did not give up. I used prayer to gain strength. I completed university with a degree in Human Resources.

The situation with my husband was still bad. I went to the police but, even after that, my husband continued to mistreat me. At one point, I slept outside with the children in the cold. But I always prayed to rebuke the wickedness around me and God did not allow me to continue to suffer.

In the middle of this difficult situation, I started asking for help so I could get away. It was difficult to get urgent support. Once again, Iris Global helped me to leave that place of confusion with my husband and find another place, to guarantee safety and peace with my children.

Papa Steve and Mana Ros received me and continued to help me with my children's health. I learned to work as a child carer (educator) at Zimpeto, and I am grateful for the attention the educators gave towards the care of my son who has special needs.

Amid all that I went through, I thank God for having graduated from university in the middle of so much "war". It was not easy for me to get here.

I thank all the leaders at Iris Global for helping me. I now want to continue with my studies and to find a good job so I can care for my family.

Thanks!

Beatriz José Timane

Stories of Hope | 111

Beatriz as a youth

Beatriz with her Mum

University graduation with Francisco and Rosa

Beatriz with her children

CHAPTER 8

César Senda

MY NAME IS César Augusto Senda. I was born on 20 June 1972.

I grew up in the Primeiro de Maio Nursery (a government orphanage in Maputo). I don't know how I got to this orphanage, because I arrived as a baby. I didn't know my father or mother and I don't know if they are alive or have passed away. I spent my early childhood at this orphanage.

When I was nine, I was transferred to the Chihango Educational Centre, another government orphanage, where I started studying from the first grade to the fifth grade. It was very difficult, as there were older people who mistreated and beat us, without anyone doing anything to stop it. Sometimes, in cold weather, they would take our blankets, and we would be left very, very cold. They told us to fight among ourselves. The Directors of the orphanage were often absent. Life was very difficult without a mother, without a father, without affection and without God.

At that time, I did not know Jesus and had not received Him as Lord and Saviour of my life. I felt very vulnerable.

In 1986, I was transferred to Centro de Salamanga, in the district of Matutuine, to continue with my studies. But I didn't even finish the year and I returned to the centre of Chihango. I fled Salamanga due to the 16-year civil war that was being fought there very intensely.

Soon after I returned to Chihango, the Mozambique government sent the military to recruit the young people who had mistreated us and abused the children. They were taken to the barracks to become soldiers. I stayed at the centre to continue with my studies.

I was transferred to an orphanage in Namaacha, where I did the 7th and 8th grades. I returned to Chihango again in 1994. I started to get very sick with gastritis problems, and I was admitted to the Central Hospital for 6 months. I had an operation due to an ulcer in my stomach. Afterwards, I was fine.

A year later, an incredible woman appeared in my life. A very special person, full of affection and love for others: Mama Aida. It was a blessing to meet her. The day I met her, my life changed completely. She introduced me to the greatest treasure and gift of my life: the Lord Jesus Christ, the Almighty.

I received Jesus Christ as Lord and Saviour of my life, and I realized that I was no longer a helpless young man, without parents, siblings or family. It was very powerful and wonderful for me to have met Mama Aida, and for her to have introduced me to Jesus.

I met my wife Rabia that same year. At first, I made her suffer a lot because I was not yet firm in Jesus. I drank, smoked cigarettes and used drugs, which resulted in me losing consciousness and mistreating her. Yet I grew strong in Jesus, and today we are a strong couple serving the Lord and our family together.

I am married, the father of six children, and we also take care of other children that the Lord has entrusted to us.

My wife is involved in a project called the Iris Agape (Love) Foundation. We work with street children and homeless children, with the aim of reintegrating these children into their families. We face great difficulties, as many of these children are born and grew up on the streets as their parents also lived on the streets. We are working to repay what someone once did for us. We love this work.

I want to thank, first of all, God, the Almighty, for everything He has done in my life. I also thank Papa Rolland and Mama Aida, Papa Steve and Mana Ros and everyone who has been part of my growth so far.

May our Lord Jesus Christ, the Almighty, bless you all. Thank you for everything.

César and Rabia

César and Rabia with his family and Mama Aida

César, Rabia and Papa Rolland

CHAPTER 9

Alberto Nuvunga

My name is Alberto Samuel Nuvunga, better known as Dalberto. I was born on 26 May 1982. I am 41 years old, and the eldest son of Samuel Alberto Nuvunga and Primina João Mbilane. I have 5 siblings: two girls and three boys.

I come from a large, poor family that depended on subsistence agriculture.

This was not easy as no one in my family worked. We lived in my grandparents' house with my aunts and uncles in the Chihango neighbourhood in the province and city of Maputo. Life was very difficult for us.

Even going to school was a big challenge, because Mozambique was in a state of civil war between 1976 and 1992. Unfortunately, the years of war were accompanied by natural calamities such as droughts and floods, and many Mozambicans like my family and I had a very bad time.

This war brought great sadness to my family because many of them died including uncles and aunts. As a family, we had to run from one side of the city to the other, being nomads for many years. But God has always been God and, according to His plans, He protected me to this day, because His grace is enough for me.

When I was eight years old, my father abandoned me and my brothers. He went to South Africa and left us without a home. Our house at the time was very small and that is where we all slept. It was made of local caniço (bamboo) material and had just collapsed because it was very weak. As my father was in South Africa, we were without any assistance. We had many needs including schooling. We were very hungry and normally had just one meal a day. These were years of drought, and our subsistence farm was not producing food.

In 1991, some men from the enemy political party (REN-AMO) moved into a nearby neighbourhood. My family and I were attacked and almost captured by them. But God protected us, and we were saved.

The very next morning, we moved again into the city where people in a church house had mercy on us and took us in. But things were even more difficult there, as twelve people were sleeping in a one-bedroom house. The important thing is that we never stopped following in God's footsteps. We were always there in church crying out for His love, which is never-ending.

God never gave up on our schooling. The enemy only attacked at night, so we continued to go to school in the day. We all studied very far away from where we lived. We had to leave the city at 3am so we could be at the school by 7.30am. After getting off the bus we had to walk 8km to school. It was a very difficult journey day after day.

In October 1992, the guns fell silent throughout Mozambique and there was peace for all Mozambicans. We returned to our original home in the Chihango neighbourhood, to find everything destroyed. We had to start all over again, and my father was far away from us. Imagine how difficult it is to live far away from your father, knowing that part of your education depends on him. It was a big challenge, and living in a post-war country was very difficult.

We started rebuilding our family farm as a basis for survival. There were some farmers who still had cattle. I had to graze the cattle to support the family while also attending fourth grade at the school in Chihango. In the morning, I would take the cattle out of the corral and then go and work on the farm with the family. In the afternoon I went to school. When I got back from school I had to collect the cattle. I did this for two years and my salary was 100 meticais per month (about $2 US). I had to use this money to help around the house and to buy shoes for school and sometimes books, because my grandparents did not always have the means to support me.

In 1994, I attended the fifth grade which was the last level of schooling at that school. I started thinking, "As this is my last class at this school, where am I going to do secondary level?" Many questions began to arise within me because my friends and neighbours became farmers after finishing fifth grade, as there were no secondary school options.

I believed God would do something for me, enabling me to continue studying. I always believed and trusted. The Bible says that God never abandons us and never fails.

So, I completed the fifth grade successfully and it was this year that Heidi and Rolland Baker, obeying the voice of God, entered Mozambique and began to do their missions work, based at Chihango.

In January 1995, registration began for the school. I wanted to go but my grandparents were always telling us, "The only thing you are going to do here is to graze cattle."

I cried so much and, finally, I spoke to my grandmother to talk to Mama Aida and Papa Rolland. Perhaps they would help me to live in their centre at Chihango and study. There was no sixth grade at the school, but I said that at least I wanted to live in the Iris centre. Finally, my grandparents understood, and spoke to Mama Aida and Papa Rolland four times.

They always said to wait but, in the end, they accepted me, and I went to the Iris centre. I was thirteen years old.

This was the year of the first miracle in my life because I received Jesus Christ as my Lord and Saviour, and by His grace I was baptised in the name of the Father, of the Son, and the Holy Spirit.

Even so, life continued to be a challenge. In February, at the beginning of the school year, I did all the morning activities, but I could not go to school because the school did not have a sixth grade. When the other children went to school I had to stay in the community. This went on for three months. In May 1996, Iris Ministries (now Iris Global) and the Government of Mozambique made an agreement that Papa Rolland, Mama Aida and all the children had to leave their centre in Chihango because the building belonged to the Mozambican Government. We were given 72 hours to leave. Mama Aida tried to explain to the leaders in Government that they were only there to help orphans and to teach God's principles, but we still had to leave. This was a time of many prayers, because we did not know where to go with the children and what to do with them all.

On the base we had weekly church services, and the wonders of God were happening in that place. We were taught to always seek Him, even when faced with turbulence. It was a very big challenge, but God continued to guide us just like He did when he led the Israelites through the desert.

In May 1996, Mama Aida and Papa Rolland took fifteen of the children and left the Chihango centre to go to live in a house in the city. I was not chosen to go with them, but I started to pray and call to God that the next group to be chosen would include me. So, a week later, on a Sunday when we were worshipping on land that had been loaned to us, there was one more selection. I was chosen to be part of the group that went to live with Mama Aida and Papa Rolland. Combined with the first group, we totalled 24 young people. We prayed every day for God to work His miracles and help us.

After two days, some missionary friends made available a children's centre called "Boa Nova" in a neighbourhood called Machava. This place had a school and church, and we were invited to join in all their activities. We felt we were a part of this family. There were about 50 boys and 30 girls, aged from four to fourteen years. We studied and worshipped, and the presence of God moved and manifested itself. We lived in that place for around a year.

The children in Boa Nova were taught to pray that all things were provided by God, and that prayer was our daily food. Indeed, God always answered our prayers, and He provided for us. I remember that some days we only had one meal, but Mama Aida and Papa Rolland encouraged us talk to God and ask Him for help.

We prayed, and He provided finances. Very soon the Ministry bought a very large plot of land in the same neighbourhood as Boa Nova, so that an Iris centre could be built at Machava. This was a miracle for us, and we all jumped for joy. It was yet another proof that God is very good.

In 1997, we left the borrowed house at Boa Nova and went to live at the Iris centre in Machava. This was not easy as it was a crowded place with many problems – yet God performed miracles almost every day. I attended seventh grade at the school on the base.

In 1999, I left the Machava centre to live in Zimpeto (a neighbouring outer suburb of Maputo). The centre at Zimpeto also had an academic school on the base. This was very good for me as, by now, I was attending eighth grade and failing, because our school in Machava did not have enough qualified teachers or classrooms and this had brought a huge setback for me.

In 2000 came many great challenges and great advances in my life. I started having a passion for praise and worship. I prayed so much about serving God, and He answered me. I started to be part of the praise and worship team. I learned to play some instruments while also attending school. God is good and I made advances in these two areas of study and worship. To this day, I am part of the Praise and Worship group in the Church centred at the Zimpeto base.

In 2004, I received very sad news about the loss of my father in South Africa. He was a victim of shooting. He was a father who left us so young, and we had no news of him during his life. For him to lose his life like this was very difficult to believe.

In the same year, I met a very beautiful woman who God had prepared for me. I had been praying for this for so long. Her name is Ivania. Everything came together and, in 2006, we entered marriage both with a ceremony with the Government and with the church. We have our own house, which is a great blessing. Ivania and I are blessed to have five very special children. They know God and follow in His footsteps, worshiping Him in spirit and truth.

In 2008, I completed twelfth grade and the following year I started trying to apply to university. I really wanted to advance my studies, which was not easy. Mozambique has few public faculties and many candidates. By the grace of the Lord, four years later, God opened the doors: with finance through Iris and the support of Papa Steve and Mana Ros, I was able to pay for a private college at one of the best Universities in Mozambique. In 2012, I graduated with a degree in public administration. I studied for four years, and God was very kind to me during this time.

Soon after, God opened the doors once again for me to continue with my studies to do a master's degree in human resources management and leadership.

This was a great challenge for me, but I managed to complete the course on time, and I am very grateful to God and to Iris Ministries. Today I have a masters in human resources management.

In 2016, God blessed me with land with the help of my family. My wife and I started a project to build a school. Initially, there were four rooms and an administrative block. In 2020, it started operating. In 2021, we had 180 students and two more classrooms. In 2022, we had 250 students and two more classrooms and, by 2023, we had 400 students and two more classrooms. We now have ten classrooms with sixteen teachers and four senior workers.

This is a great blessing for my family and the Mozambican community.

Today I work at the Iris Global centre in Zimpeto as an advisor to the National Administrator, Francisco Mandlate. I am also the overseer of our university students – currently numbering 35. I lead our worship teams, who do more than five services each week.

All of this has been a great opportunity for my growth in God. I am thankful for everything that Iris Global has done for my family. It has been a great learning experience for me. I am a person who, today, can testify to the greatness of God, who is always good.

I am thankful for all the teaching and support given to me and my family by Mama Aida and Papa Rolland, Mana Ros and Papa Steve, and all the community of Iris Global.

Today I am a mature man, and my life is a testimony to the goodness of God. I want to be a good example to all Mozambicans.

Dalberto with wife Vania and children

University graduation

Dalberto enjoying ice cream

CHAPTER 10

Francisco Mandlate

My name is Francisco José Mandlate. I am 47 years old. I was born on the 3 June 1976 in Manhiça, a Southern District of Mozambique in Maputo Province. It is primarily an agricultural District.

My mother is a housewife and a farmer. My father was working for the Government at the Ministry of Defence. He is now deceased.

I started school in Manhiça when I was six years old. School was about thirty minutes' walk from home, but that was the closest school for my house. My father was working in Maputo City and would come home every Friday and leave the first thing Monday morning, so I only saw him at weekends. During the week, I was with my mother, my older sister and a lot more relatives - maybe five more people - cousins and other relatives.

While I was still in first grade in Manhiça, Civil war started: the war between the Government and RENAMO (the opposition political party), and things started to be complicated for us.

I remember that, on two occasions, the Renamo Rebels came to our house in Manhiça in the evening, demanding that we give them food. I remember that we did not have any food to give to them. Fortunately, these were the first days of the war, so they were not yet aggressive, and did not do any harm to us.

The second time they came to our house it was almost midnight, and this time they were more aggressive. Even though they did not do us any harm, their behaviour was inappropriate, and this made us to think twice about staying in Manhiça.

Every night we would go to sleep in the bush, in fear that they would come for things and food, and, if we did not give it to them, maybe one day they could harm us. They started kidnapping people to join them, and took young boys to be soldiers, so we had to leave Manhiça and come to live with our father in Maputo in his work residence. We stayed with him till I was nine years old, when my father was forced to leave Mozambique, due to conflicts that he had with the Government at the time. He left us behind, and we stayed at his work residence till we were kicked out, since my father was not with the Government any longer.

Life became more complicated for us, as we had nowhere to stay, no food, and my mother was uneducated, so she could not work. She started a very small business, but it was not enough to feed us. At this point, the war was getting worse, and everything was difficult for us. My mother had to go back to Manhiça to stay with my aunt, and I had to stay behind in Maputo, with nowhere to stay and no food. I was taken to Swaziland (now called Eswatini) to a refugee camp where Mozambican victims of war were taken, since it was not safe to be in Maputo, and going back to Manhiça was not an option for young boys at the time.

The refugee camp was in in a District called Malindza. I started school again there. It was difficult for me because of the language: Swati and English, no Portuguese, so I had to start in grade one but, after a few months, I was moved to grade three because I picked up English and Swati in a very short time.

This is where I met Jesus, in School in Swaziland. I was approached by one of my teachers who spoke to me about Jesus. My father and mother were Catholics, so I used to attend church with them, but I did not really know Jesus as my Saviour and King. I was enrolled in this teacher's group of drama and dance, and in this group, I learned more about Jesus because most of the dramas and songs were Christian. I started to attend a Baptist Church in the refugee camp and became an active member and then I was baptised.

Despite being at a refugee camp in a foreign country, I was at peace when I received Jesus, but life was not easy for me: a very young boy in a foreign country and with no one to take care of me. I relied on church members, and moved to stay at the pastoral house, to take care of the church: cleaning, preparing the church for the sermons and doing whatever needed to be done at the church.

School was going well, and I was progressing well but, on the other hand, my mother, my older sister, and two of my younger brothers were back in Mozambique. War was at its peak, and danger was imminent, so I was not at peace when I thought about them. My elder sister had to start working as a maid when she was only fourteen years old, and my mother had to try to sell whatever she could to feed them. The war lasted for sixteen years. This is a very long time to be living in a war zone, but there was no other option for them. When the war ended, I had to go back to Mozambique. At that time, I was in seventh grade in Swaziland.

Preparations started for all the Mozambican refugees to return home, including me. We were repatriated back to Mozambique but, when I got to Maputo, I could not find my mother or my brothers. They were all living in Manhiça with my aunt, but I could not go to Manhiça and stay with them, because my aunt already had many people in her house. So, I had to stay in Maputo with one of my uncles, who himself was struggling in life, but luckily, he agreed to take me into his house. At the time, he was separated from his wife. She had gone back home to her parents, taking all her children, so he was alone and could take me in. After some months, they got back together, and his wife brought back all her children and there was no more space for me to sleep. Luckily, I could still eat there, but I could not sleep there. The only option for me was to go and sleep at another of my aunts, who also lived in Maputo, but in a different area. This meant that I had to walk about thirty minutes or more to go to school and sleep every day for many years: eat in one area and go to sleep in a different area.

At the time that this was happening, I was praying to the Lord Jesus to change things. The other challenge was that in Swaziland, where I started schooling, everything was in English and Swati, but now back home, everything was in Portuguese. What a predicament. I was enrolled in eighth grade in a Christian school in Maputo and I restarted schooling. Luckily, one of my cousins took me to town and I saw the Baptist Church, so we went there to meet the Pastor. I began attending this church and started to do some small jobs, including interpreting when there were visiting missionaries at the church.

My church work used to involve me going to various Government agencies and, one of those days, I went to the Immigration office where I met a South African Missionary called Mark Harper. He was having problems understanding the Immigration officers. I helped him with interpretation, and he then said he wanted me to help him start his organisation in Maputo called Youth for Christ. I told him to come with me to meet my Pastor who OK'd his request, and I started working with this organisation in Maputo. However, his office was in Matola, maybe one hour's drive (by car) from where I was living, but the bus journey involved two buses. I did not have enough money to take two buses to go and work there every day, so I had to wake up very early - 3 am - and walk half the distance to take only one bus. This was not an easy thing to do, since I had to walk maybe two or more hours to get to the next bus stop so that I could be on time for the bus and get to Matola.

At this new organisation, I started getting a salary that was 200 meticais in the Mozambican currency (about $4US) a month. Not much, but good for me at that time.

While working for Youth for Christ in Matola, I got to know Iris Ministries when the Ministry had just begun in 1995 in Chihango. I started doing some volunteer work with them, but in the name of Youth for Christ. I met Heidi Baker, who liked my work as a volunteer and asked me to join them. I agreed to join Iris Ministries in October 1998. At the time, I was still attending Secondary school. I was in eighth grade and Iris Ministries encouraged me to carry on studying.

Now, from my house to Iris Ministries it was only a one hour walk, and maybe fifteen minutes' drive, but I did not want to spend any money on transport. I wanted the money that I was now earning to go towards building a house, because I did not have any place to stay that was secure. At Iris, they were now giving me a sum of 420 Mets a month, which was double the amount I had been getting in Matola, and I did not have to use any of the money for a bus.

One of my uncles had a very old house in Choupal that was almost abandoned due to its condition. He told my mother that she could use the house, so my mother told me I could stay there. I was very glad to move to this house alone, aged just 17. This was because I was not comfortable where I had been staying, since I had to eat in one place and go to sleep in a different area.

At the time, I did not understand why all these things were happening to me, but now I do get the big picture: the Lord Jesus Christ was preparing me for greater things. He was showing me that from the dust He can raise men who will represent His glory in this world, especially in Mozambique. Just like many great prophets and men of God, such as Joseph, who - from the pit that he was put in - ascended to be a great Governor in a foreign land. God prepared Joseph first, so now I do understand what the Lord was doing in my life. He was preparing me for what was about to come.

At Iris, I started working in the school as a teacher, but the school was not yet registered, and the Ministry of Education wanted to come to do an inspection to register it. At the time, the existing School Director did not have anyone to meet with this team of inspectors. I was called in to welcome them, and to answer all their questions. Thanks to the Lord, this is what I did, and the school was approved.

From this time on, Heidi Baker wanted me to help the former Iris Director in administration, so I did. She also chose me to be her personal assistant, and I did this for many years till she moved to Pemba. Heidi then appointed me to be the Administrator of the Organisation, a role which I also accepted. At this time, I worked alongside Steven and Rosalind Lazar, the Iris Ministries Directors at Zimpeto, and I have been working with them ever since. These Directors changed my life dramatically, since they showed me the way forward with life: not just to depend on your existing salary but also to think outside the box.

I married a beautiful young lady called Rosa, in 2001. We dated for almost seven years before marriage. Rosa's family thought we were taking a very long time, and we are still happy today because we followed His timing and guidance.

Rosa and I started a decoration business, and, from this business, the Lord blessed us. We started building slowly, but surely. I had promised myself that my future children would not experience the same thing that I did: having to stay in one area during the day and sleep in a different area at night.

Talking about children, in Africa, when you get married, you expect to have children, but that did not happen to us. We visited many doctors in Mozambique and South Africa for more than 10 years, and nothing. This was very frustrating, because I was asking the Lord, "Why us? Why can't we have children?" And no answer. God was blessing us in other areas, but not giving us children. We tend to forget the good things that the Lord is doing for us and only concentrate on what He is *not* doing, so frustration settles in our lives. I started not to trust the Lord entirely, thinking that He was not able to solve all our problems.

After some time, I told myself that His answer on children was no, so I would adopt a child, to help children that did not have parents and for us to have a child. So, we adopted a little girl, called Lesley. At the time, she was only two months old. We took her to our house, loved her and took very good care of her. Unfortunately, four months after adopting Lesley we learned that she was HIV positive. We accepted that, and took her for consults every month but, after twelve years, she passed away due to HIV. This was a very, very sad moment of my life. I thought maybe the Lord did not want us to have children, end of story. But as time went on, I began to think again about Joseph in the Bible. He was a very good servant of God who lost everything, and then the Lord gave him back even greater things. I made peace with God and now I am once more at peace with God and love Him whatever happens. He is the Lord, always.

I went on with my studies, doing a university degree with the support of Iris Global. I finished that course and went on to do a Master's in public administration. I also finished that, and now I am doing a Doctorate, slowly but surely. All of this is thanks to the Lord, and to Iris Global.

At the same time, Rosa and I carried on with another business, building houses and renting them out. Now we have about five houses that we are renting and all of them belong to us. This is a very big achievement in Mozambique. God is blessing us a lot.

In my work here at Iris Global, I have said previously that I started as a simple teacher, but the Lord lifted me up to be the National Administrator of this great Ministry and again - from the dust - He took me to be with Kings and Presidents. I can sit at the same table with them, I can pick up a phone and call a President, a mayor and many influential people in the Government. This is what the Lord was preparing me for. He wanted to show me that from a very poor background, He can lift me up to meet important people, and to be part of the decision-making people of Mozambique.

Now my business is growing, and my family is happy, because we have just adopted a young girl called Nhelety, a sweet girl from the Zimpeto centre. Now she has a family, and we also have a wonderful daughter, so the Lord always gives you back what you lose.

As for sleeping in one area and eating in another, now that is finished because I have houses that I can give to my children so that they will not suffer like I did.

I thank God for shaping me to be the man that I am now, confident and willing to learn and to do more when the Lord tells me to. Now I consider myself to be really blessed. This is because I have a wonderful family and a good house, we have food every day on our table and our children can eat whatever we can provide for them.

Rosa and I have been married for 23 years, although it seems like yesterday. Our marriage is firm and strong despite the challenges we have faced, like losing our daughter Lesley in 2018. This is still a very sad situation for us. Yet the Lord is gracious to us. Rosa has a wonderful job at the Government, and she has been promoted to be the Chief of Finances at the Attorney Generals' office in Maputo, with a good salary. This is a miracle for us. Indeed, the Lord did prepare us for greater things.

Francisco and Rosa

Family photo

Francisco and his Mum

CHAPTER 11

Hermínio Muchave

My name is Hermínio José Muchave. I am one of seven siblings, and the first and only son of my father. My mother and father met when my father was doing mandatory military service in 1986 in the city of Chimoio, and on 13 March 1988, the cutest baby in Southern Africa was born. I have in total three brothers, and three sisters. Unfortunately, all my brothers have died, and it is now just me and my three sisters.

My childhood was full of suffering. I passed through hard situations that I would not wish for any other child. Things were going well until I was two years old, but then my parents separated and then the suffering in my life began. My stepmother – whose name I no longer remember - was living with my dad. She was so mean and did not give me food. Whenever my dad was at work, she used to put cooking oil on my lips at lunchtime, so when my dad came home from work for lunch, he would think I'd eaten. I couldn't tell the truth because I would get beaten by my stepmother as soon as my dad returned to work.

End of the world

One of the episodes that marked me very much was the New Year's Eve of 1999-2000. In Mozambique, New Year's Eve and New Year's Day are always celebrated with great enthusiasm and celebration. No matter how poor a family was, at that time of year families would make sure they had at least chicken, chips, rice, cakes and drinks for the party. I do not know if it was like this all over the world, but in Mozambique there were rumours that the year 2000 would be the end of the world. Some people sold their belongings, people in the countryside sold and killed their animals, and there was a lot of waste. I cannot tell you where this information came from. Maybe it was because humanity was going to reach a big milestone, but many people in Mozambique took it seriously.

Even with many people squandering lots of food, my family and I were still at rock bottom, with no way out. Our situation was still the same, and I remember that New Year's Eve as if it were yesterday. I do not remember the meal we had. I just remember that my mother only had enough to buy a small bottle of coke which three people shared. That was one of the times where I felt in my skin the pain of being poor. I do not even want to imagine what thoughts were going through my mother's head, because it must be painful when a mother can't provide for her children. My hope was that better days would come. I just could not imagine how.

Many years later, when I came to the United States, one of the things that I noticed is how many of the restaurants and fast-food places have refill systems for all the drinks, and that just reminded me of that 1999 New Year's Eve when we only had one Coke for three people.

Year 2000

The Year 2000 was very challenging for the southern part of Mozambique. The year began with heavy and intense rain, many areas were flooded, roads and infrastructures were destroyed, and people lost their property. It seemed that we were living in the end of the world. Our situation showed no signs of improvement and, if someone told me I would be where I am today, I swear I would have not believed it, because we were in so much trouble. If it were not for my mother's family, who did not get tired of continuously helping us, our situation could have been much worse.

It was in the same year that I received the sad news that my father had died. This news only worsened my situation and my dream of maybe one day going to school and becoming a person of value. My father had not given any assistance, and we had not seen each other for a long time, but just knowing that I *had* a father gave me a little comfort and hope that one day things would change for the better.

Since we had returned from Chimoio, I had the opportunity to meet him twice. The first time, I remember, was on the street. He asked me why I ran away from home. He seemed to be sad with me. I want to imagine that deep in his heart, he was happy to see me and to know that I was in good health. As far as I know, I am my father's only son and, in Africa - Mozambique in particular - the father wants to have a son to continue the family's name. The second time I saw him was at his house, where he lived with another woman. This was the last time I saw him. The house was very run down, and he was already a little weakened with signs of tuberculosis.

The woman who lived with my dad gave us the sad news that he was sick and had been admitted to the Machava hospital. We quickly prepared a meal for him, and rushed to the hospital but, when we arrived, after so much urgency, we were given the sad news: he had lost his life 5 days ago, and because no one went there to identify and claim the body, he was buried in the mass grave. We had been hoping to see him and take care of him, but it was too late, and the saddest thing is that we were not able to have a dignified funeral for him.

At the time, I was sad and so was my mom. They were not together, but I guess she was worried about me growing up without my father. Now when I remember it, I get very sad. I wanted so badly to have my father with me. I always wanted to have someone to call father and to share all my moments, good and bad. I have even thought about the possibility of being adopted, because I did not live with my father, and he died when I was young.

All my childhood I had to go through moments of hardship. Our family has always been disorganized and dysfunctional, and this made it difficult for me and my brothers to face life with great courage and confidence, because it is in the family where our fears and insecurity are safely exposed. Family provides security, and it is a perfect place to make mistakes, because we are surrounded by people who love us and want our best. They serve as the foundation for our success. That is the foundation my siblings and I did not have as kids and in our pre-teens.

Iris Global Zimpeto

Arco-Iris (meaning rainbow in English) is used to symbolize a new era, a new beginning. Fate would have it that *my* new beginning was in the month of March 2001, when my mother took me, my sisters Zaida and Onesia, and my brother Hilário to the Zimpeto centre in Maputo. I remember when we got there, Mama Aida was handing out gifts to all the children: the residents of the orphanage and the non-residents. There were more than 500 children from the centre and the outsiders as well. My mother had come to ask for information on the requirements needed for my siblings and me to be admitted. The response was not positive, because the centre was super-crowded, but we were lucky and privileged to receive gifts from the hands of Mama Aida. This was the first time that my siblings and I had ever received gifts and, for me it worked well, because March is my birthday month.

At the time I had no idea what was going on but, today, I can look back and see God orchestrating His plan in my life. It was an unforgettable day. My brothers and I got many gifts, something we never imagined happening. I could not contain the emotion, because God had already drafted my story, and it did not stop there: there was another box of surprises to open.

We were not accepted to live in the centre because the place was overcrowded but, on the same day, we heard that we *were* allowed to attend the school at Zimpeto, despite not having any documents, (my mother had lost all our personal documents). My older brother entered the fifth grade, I entered the second grade, and my younger sister was in the first grade. At that time, my education level was zero. I only didn't start in the first grade because I thought: "If I start in the first grade together with my younger sister, she will not respect me because we will be in the same class, and I am much older."

The fact that the center was overcrowded was not the only reason we were not admitted. Between 1992 and 1997, in Maputo particularly, there were rumors of white people kidnapping/trafficking children to sell them elsewhere, and many families were afraid that something bad would happen to their children. When we arrived at the center, the one thing that caught our attention was the presence of many white people, and then my older brother remembered the saying, "Tata mama, tata papa" which means "Goodbye mom, goodbye dad." He ruled out the possibility of living in the center because he was afraid of being kidnapped. He said to the administrators that he did not want to stay in the centre. He also thought that my mother was throwing us away, and that is what it looked like at that moment.

In the week after starting school, we did not see our brother. We only saw him two weeks later, when he came to visit us, bringing lots of stuff with him. He had been accepted into the orphanage, having had help from some of his classmates who lived there. One of those young people was called Florindo. We could not believe what we heard, but it was the truth. Our brother had become direct friends with Mama Aida, and the ghosts of "Tata mama, tata papa" had already disappeared.

That is the power of love. Mama Aida and Papa Rolland are amazing people. They love without reservations and give without counting the cost. It was this love that softened my brother's heart. He came home clean, with new clothes, new shoes, and many other things. We thank God that he did not forget us. During the year 2001 until the beginning of 2002, he came to visit us at least once a month. On many of these visits, he brought with him things to share with us. Of all that he received, he kept a part for us, and his visit to our home was always a cause for joy.

By this time, we started to smell something positive coming in our direction. We could already see a light at the end of the tunnel: something was going to work out.

"Hoyo-hoyo!" ("Welcome!") That is how we were greeted when we arrived for the second time at Iris Global Zimpeto. This time we were there to stay. My brother Hilario became our hero when, through his influence with Mama Aida, he managed to get a signature from her that authorised us to stay in the orphanage. My brother was an outgoing person who caught the attention of anyone who crossed his way.

Once again, I want to underline that our arrival at Iris Zimpeto was in March, my birthday month. We were warmly welcomed, and given new clothes, new shoes and new blankets. Everything for me was new. I could not contain the joy of having a bed that was just for me, a shower, a toilet and much more. You will not believe that having electricity was also new to me.

At Zimpeto, we had three meals a day. When I was growing up, having three meals a day was not for any family. Most families had only two meals: a late breakfast and a dinner that was *sacred*. From dinner you took the famous "Xiquento". (This is the name given to leftover food that is usually served to the little ones while waiting for breakfast.) At Zimpeto, everything was new to me, and to this day, everything continues to be new.

I do not know how to explain it, and I still do not have the words to thank God for everything He has done for me, and everything He is doing to this very day. He was very generous with me, using people like Mama Aida, Papa Rolland, Mana Ros and Papa Steve, missionary Célia Mendes, educators like Master Julio and others. I am always amazed to see where God has allowed me to go. He has taken me out of the position of asking and put me in the position of giving. I have learned that giving is better than receiving.

For the first few weeks of living in the centre, I felt like a fish out of water. A fish is very dependent on the environment in which it lives, and when it comes out of the water it dies. It did not take me long to realize that I was out of my normal habitat. I had more than 500 brothers and sisters, instead of two or three brothers. In a brief time, I had to undo the habits and customs I brought from home. At first it was a great challenge, because many of the boys in my dormitory came from the street and had a way of being that I had never seen before. They did not see a difference between good and evil. Many of them had spent almost all their childhood in the streets of the city of Maputo. Facing this situation, I had to make a choice that no one could make for me: to endure that situation and enjoy so many other benefits, or to return to my home and be without school and without decent living conditions.

It did not take long for me to start making friends. I had three friends: Florêncio, Luís and Tomás Nhanhane. Nhanhane means bird in Changana (the local tribal language). He ran so much. I remember being together on the athletics team representing our school and whenever it was time to race, he would win first place. To us he did not run, he *flew*. Tomás was a strategic friend as he worked in the kitchen, and I would get extra food when I needed. I also created friendships with other boys and educators (carers in our dormitories) and became familiar with their way of being. I learned to understand them and love them as they were. They were not bad at all. They were just boys who had gone through a lot in life.

I started studying when I was 13 years old and entered the second grade. My first classroom was a "dorm-class": in the morning it was used as a classroom and in the afternoon, it continued as a dormitory. In my first three months of this class, I found it hard to understand the work, and often resorted to asking a classmate, Alberto, to explain things to me and help me with homework.

I was so thirsty to learn that, in less than four months, I was already beginning to assimilate things. I remember that in the last three months of the classes, I was an A student, and my friend Alberto was the one who came to *me* to ask for help with homework.

Towards the end of the year, I began to participate in the youth group, which was led by Pastor Norberto Sango, who was also the leader of the worship team. He was very influential with the youth. By this time, I was already participating in the Church services - this was my first contact with an evangelical church. Early the following year, 2003, I accepted Jesus as my Lord and Saviour and was baptised in the month of March during a national conference of the Partners in Harvest church linked with the ministry. At the end of 2003, I began to participate in discipleship training, which was taught by a Brazilian missionary named Célia Mendes. In this discipleship, I learned the basic principles of Christianity: to love God above all things, to love my neighbor as myself, and to forgive others as I have been forgiven. I learned to walk on my own feet, carrying my cross and following Jesus.

So, while I took my first steps in school, I also took my first steps in Christian life. I had so much desire to be able to grow in fearing God, in loving Him, and in loving my neighbour. At the same time, the desire to be able to learn more in school and be better than in the previous year was greater. So much so that, in 2003, I came second in my class and, in 2004, when I did the fourth grade, I came first. I received a gift from the hands of Mama Aida: a ball. I was incredibly happy with that.

One of the great challenges I had in my first four years at the orphanage was ignoring the taunts. The boys teased so much. I did not know how to ignore it, and it all ended in fighting. I struggled with fighting at school. I struggled with fighting in the dorm. I fought all the time. By 2005, I was tired of all the fighting, so I decided to stop. In prayer, I asked God to help me not to fight anymore - to help me endure all the provocations. By then I knew more about the word of God and could already assure myself a little when I was provoked, but my desire was to stop completely. (I was also responsible for discipleship groups, and I wanted to set a good example for those boys.) I had no idea what God was going to do. The fights stopped not only in my life but in the lives of all the children of the orphanage. 2008 was the year I noticed that almost no children fought in the orphanage: the children argued, but rarely fought. To me, this was clearly a miracle of God.

It is customary for African families to have expectations that, when their children are grown up, they can support them in some way: financially, morally, etc. With me it was no different: I just did not expect it to be so early. I was not working. I was also being supported by Iris Global. Without much room to manoeuvre, my mother had these expectations of me. In 2006, I heard that my mother's little house had burned down. I told my missionary mentor, Célia Mendes, about this, and the ministry helped build a new house for my mother (even though they were already helping us). I was very grateful for that gesture. At this time, I shared with my mother what I was learning in discipleship about forgiveness and love for others, as I felt this was what my family needed.

In 2004, I was separated from my brothers and sister. My younger sister was taken to Pemba and my older brother to Beira. It was difficult for me because these were the only people who understood me better and being away from them seemed more like a punishment for me. Even though I was sad with this situation, I had to continue with my life. I decided to focus on myself and give my best to get good results in school and to be able to stay at Zimpeto. (The centre had begun a reintegration program with the aim of returning children to families. This was because Iris Global has always believed that the best place for the child is with the family unless the child had no family member who could support them. Sometimes, the Ministry was forced to reintegrate children whose behaviour was damaging other children and no-one wanted to be reintegrated for *that* reason.) I did not want to be reinstated to my family yet, because I wanted to enjoy all that God had for me through Iris Global.

Step by step I was growing, gaining a little spiritual, psychological, and physical maturity. The centre entrusted me with some responsibilities, leading cleaning groups, home group, and even giving me responsibility as an assistant to the dorm parents working at weekends, taking care of around thirty children.

In 2010, I reached a big milestone in my life. I finished high school. I could not believe that a child who started studying at the age of 13 could achieve this, while my cousin - who was a year older than me was doing sixth grade. Prior to going to school, I could not read or print my own name. To be finishing high school in ten years was a great privilege and honour for me. For some this might seem normal but, inside my heart, I just had to thank God and Iris Global for giving me the opportunity to dream.

That same year I was invited by Vovote Emílio to be part of the worship team. Before joining this group, I already served in church, sweeping and cleaning pews and singing praise songs during the services. I told the leader that I did not know how to play guitar or any other instrument, but this was fine with him. He wanted me to learn to play the guitar so I could lead worship whenever it was needed. He gave me plenty of time to do so. At that time, I could only play one song - Heart of Worship - in the key of "D". After a few months, he told me that I was going to lead the following week. I confess that I was afraid of not being able to, or of playing the wrong chords. Thank God, I had support from the whole group, and everything worked out. To this day, God has given me the grace to continue to lead praise and worship for hundreds of people in various parts of the world.

In 2011, I was unable to go to university for several reasons. I was entrusted with more responsibilities on the centre. I started supervising the library during the summer holidays and I worked in the Hospitality area. I was the first Mozambican to be part of the Hospitality team, and it was at this time that I developed more of my English in speaking and writing, because many of our visitors spoke English. I went on to lead the hospital ministry, visiting the sick in hospitals and leading worship in the church.

2012 started well. I started university, another great milestone in my life. The boy who had no dreams and who had started studying at the age of 13 had now chosen the direction to follow in his life. Financial Management and Banking. Yet, in Mozambique we have a saying that goes: "The joy of the poor does not last long." This time the problem was not poverty: it was something deeper and very sad.

The saddest news of my life came to us from the Central Hospital. My brother, my hero, Hilário, lost his life – a victim of prolonged illness. Another tragedy for me and my family. He died incredibly early, only 27 years old. I am 35 now and I feel young with a lot of energy. He was involved in the music industry. He had over 15 songs on the market, and he was still emerging. It was a great loss. We were the only men in our family, and it brought a lot of balance in the middle of four women. His early departure left me with a lot of responsibility for my sisters and my mother. More than that, the loss of my brother left a big void in my heart. I liked him very much and, despite being a little distant, we had good chemistry. Since the tragedy of his death in March 2012, I have often thought about what life would be like if my brother was alive. I have dreamed of him hundreds of times. Today, I can only be grateful for everything my brother did for me and my family.

Life had to go on for me. I had to somehow find the energy to be able to continue to fight, and to believe that one day God would put a smile back on my lips again. After the death of my brother, I had some relapses in my personal life. I made many mistakes that I am not proud of. The only thing I did not fail to do was to always cry out to God, like a sheep falling into the mud. It helped so much that I had the Iris Global family by my side, and my own family also giving me a lot of support.

In 2015, after 13 years in the centre, I was reintegrated by mutual consent to my own house, which Iris Global had bought for me in 2009. I was returning to a life that was new. Everything I knew was related to my life in Zimpeto. Now I had to learn to live in the community. Once again, I felt like a fish out of water. In the same year of 2015, I finished my studies at Unitiva University.

In 2017, three major events happened in my life: God had not forgotten me. On 2 June I graduated with a bachelor's degree as a Financial and Banking Manager. On 30 June my marriage proposal was accepted and on 30 September I got married to Kasey DeMars, my beautiful sparkling wife. Five years later, after many attempts, God blessed us with an exceptionally beautiful girl, our Princess Sophia.

If, in 2001, someone had said that I, a 13-year-old boy with no dreams, who could not read or print his own name, would – in 16 years - have a bachelor's degree, would be speaking and writing in English and would be married to a beautiful American woman, I would have said 1000 times over that this was impossible. I am still amazed for what God did in my life through Iris Global. They were God's hands to me.

If you ask me what God's deposit in my life was, I will undoubtedly say that it was the generosity of people. The first example was my uncle Zeca Duque, and aunt Isabel Duque and their family. Without hesitation, they welcomed us to their home in the city of Chimoio in 1993, when my mother was looking for better living conditions. They took care of us without getting tired. They bought a house, and they became our refuge. We could not have stayed six years if it were not for them. They made our life easier, and their seven children treated us with great affection and love. They were the first angels of God in our life.

The second act of generosity was shown to me and my siblings by Mama Aida and Papa Rolland, who, through their Iris Global ministry, gave us shelter and school and gave us the opportunity to dream. In 1994, when they read in the newspaper that Mozambique was one of the poorest countries in the world after just having come out of a 16-year civil war, they packed their bags and travelled to Mozambique. They gave everything they had, so that thousands of children in Mozambique and beyond could have opportunities to go to school and have bread on the table. Through their obedience to God, they have impacted many people today in Mozambique, and other countries in Africa. Communities have been transformed in numerous ways, including the provision of water boreholes, and the construction of maternity hospitals, clinics, and schools. They were the second angels sent by God to take care of us.

The third act of generosity was shown to me by Papa Steve and Mana Ros Lazar, who for more than 20 years dedicated their lives to serve Iris Global Zimpeto. They had a stable and comfortable life with their family in Australia but were driven by a desire to contribute to a better world. They shared everything they had with the Zimpeto base, serving children and local communities, building schools, and providing shelter for orphans, the elderly, and widows. Mana Ros has a heart for babies and children. Papa Steve also loves children and babies and - more than that - he has a heart for teenagers and young people. He did an excellent job with young people of my generation. I must confess that we were not malleable people. We gave them a lot of work, but Papa Steve was like a father, always patient, and looking for our best in all situations. He was slow to anger and quick to forgive. These were the third angels sent by God into my life.

After everything I have said about my life, who I was and who I am today, I feel within me that generosity is the mark of ministry that God has for me while I am on this earth. Just as God did to me: putting people in my life who planted seeds of generosity; people who gave me so much love; people who cared for me and my family when we were at rock bottom; people I consider my heroes. I now just want to return the favour.

After 22 years, I feel that God is putting in me the desire to do something to help people who find themselves in the same situation as I was. Walking today in some neighborhoods of the city of Maputo or Matola, I see people and families in need, and this reminds me of where God took me from. I do not have much, but the little my family has, we want to share with those who have nothing. My heart weeps and makes me want to help everyone. I pray to God that my acts of generosity will make a difference in people's lives. I also pray that God will raise up other people who are generous to share some of what they have with others.

Now, this is what I am doing. I went from being fatherless to being a father to many children in America and Mozambique. My wife and I are involved with foster care in the United States, and we have had nine children in our home so far. When we are in Mozambique, we serve as missionaries at Iris Global Zimpeto, caring for children at the center, in the community and ministering at the local church. I do not think I would be doing what I am doing now if it wasn't for my past. Through my suffering God gave me passion for those who are in need. I thank God for His work in me.

My wife and I returned to the USA in 2021 for Kasey to complete her midwifery training. In late 2023 Papa Steve invited us to return to Iris Global Zimpeto to take on the role as Children's Director. Kasey, Sophia and I arrived in June 2024 and have committed to two years (minimum) in this role.

God is good - ALL THE TIME

Hermínio University graduation

Hermínio, Kasey and Sophia

Hermínio with his family and Mum

CHAPTER 12

Hilda Francisco

My name is Hilda Francisco. I was born on 3 May 1989, in Maputo, Mozambique. I am currently living in the neighbourhood of Zimpeto.

I'm not an experienced writer and my first language is not English. I hope my story makes sense and touches your heart. I can't remember many things from my past, but I pray my story may give God glory.

Before coming to live at the Zimpeto base of Iris Ministries, I lived with my mother (Alice Fernando Magaia) and my four siblings in terrible conditions: a one-bedroom caniço (bamboo) house, with a small living room.

My parents separated when I was three years old, and at that time my mother returned, with us, to my grandparents' house, where she started life again. Sometime later, my father decided to leave the place of my birth. He went to live in another province with another woman and never wanted to know about us.

There were more than twenty people living at my grandparents' house. At mealtimes it was difficult to eat, because there was not enough food for everyone. My mother would often go without food and give us her meals.

Seeing that we were suffering a lot at our grandparents' house, my mother decided to leave and went to the area chief (a representative for the local area) of another neighbourhood. She asked him for a plot of land, and said she would pay later.

The local leaders of the area had compassion on my mother and gave her land, where she built a caniço house with one-bedroom and a living room. So, we were able to move there, despite not having anything to start life over.

My mother did not have a formal job, but with the grace of God, she managed to buy what was needed for the house. She did little odd jobs such as work in other people's vegetable plots and, in this way, earned a little money to support us. At other times, she would go into the bush and cut wood, and then go and sell the wood from house to house.

In our house, we only had one meal a day, and we often shared our one plate amongst two or three of us. Our life was not a bed of roses and we were in need.

The years went by and, when I turned seven years old, I went to school to attend the 1st class. That's when my mother learned that there was a church near home called Partners in Harvest, and decided that the whole family should attend services. It was at this moment that we met Mama Aida and Papa Rolland. They were founders of the church, and the school where I studied was an old government centre that they had renovated and were using to house children who were orphaned or abandoned.

When I turned nine, I was in third grade, and life at home got worse and worse because my mother started having health problems due to the heavy work she did. She could no longer support us, let alone pay the school's expenses. One Sunday, she talked to the pastor of the church and asked him to speak to Mama Aida to take us into the centre at Zimpeto.

One beautiful Sunday, Mama Aida came to the church with other missionaries and was ministering the Word of God. After the service was over the pastor took my mother and they went to talk to Mama Aida about my mother's request to take us into Zimpeto due to our living conditions. She was moved by our story and agreed to take me and my two siblings.

We had to say goodbye to our mother in the church, because they took us on the same day to the Children's centre in Zimpeto. The farewell was so painful, and I cried a lot because, for the first time, I was going to be away from my mother. But I didn't know that God was opening a way for me. I arrived at the centre in May 1999, and it was very difficult to adapt to the new environment. I remember crying day and night and wanting to go home because I missed my mother.

When I arrived at the centre I was given new clothes, a toothbrush, and new shoes. This was very exciting because I had never received new clothes. (At home it was normal to go one year or more without having new clothes. My mother's greater concern was to have food on the table). The next day I went to school and there I received school supplies and was welcomed by my classmates.

A week later, my mother came to visit us at the centre. I thought she'd come to pick us up, but that wasn't so. I didn't hold back and started crying again, because I thought she didn't want us anymore.

As time went on, I realized that my mother had to admit us to the centre because she couldn't take care of all of us. In the centre, I had a good education, I had three meals a day, I received good care, and I had enough clothes. My mother visited regularly.

In the girls' area, there were nine bedrooms for more than

100 girls. There were not enough beds for all of us and we had to sleep two girls in each bed.

We all used the same bathrooms, so it took us a long time to shower, but compared to the life that I lived at home, this was luxury. Every day we had three meals (breakfast, lunch and dinner).

In my childhood, I spent a lot of time alone in my thoughts. I liked to sing, read, interpret, and make up my own poems and songs. I did not imagine that living in the Iris Global centre at Zimpeto would completely change my life.

When I was 13 years old, I was baptised by Mama Aida and the pastors of the church in Zimpeto. It was a special day for me because I gave my life to Jesus.

The years went by, and I started singing in church in the worship group. God began to give me new songs and I started writing. I love to hear God's voice at times when I am feeling alone. In 2001 at the age of 17, I met Papa Steve and Mana Ros.

In 2003, Mama Aida and Papa Rolland moved to Pemba in the North of Mozambique and Papa Steve and Mana Ros were appointed as the new Directors of the centre in Zimpeto.

I was so impacted by them, and I think they liked me at first glance too. I experienced so many emotions at Iris Global. This was my family, but I never forgot where I came from.

In early 2011, the centre built a house for me in the local area close to the centre, and there I was reintegrated (reintegration is a term we use for returning children to the community, perhaps to a family member, or a pastor or carer. For older children it may be a house by themselves).

I started working in the kitchen at Iris Global so I could afford my daily expenses. That year I finished my Grade 12 studies and then I entered the university, which was another challenge for me.

Author's note *(This was a huge achievement. Hilda was one of the first girls from our centre to complete Grade 12 and gain admission to university.)*

I wanted to study to become "someone" in the future. Some said that studying was crazy, but for me it was a gift. I heard from many that my life would end badly because I would rebel and end up alone (the culture in Mozambique was for girls of 18 to get married and begin a family). Much time has now passed, and my life is like a book. Each chapter is a new beginning. Each new beginning is a challenge and each challenge an achievement. In each conquest is a new way of seeing life and making everything worthwhile.

In 2014, I got married to Antonio in the church, and today we have two beautiful daughters.

In 2017, I had an unexpected encounter with my father. My brothers and I decided to go looking for him. We went to the province of Gaza where he lived with his other family. It was a reunion full of many emotions. He asked for forgiveness for what had occurred, although nothing will erase the bad impression. I have of him because he left us in misery. I was able to forgive him because God taught me to love and forgive my neighbour.

Now I can say that miracles really do exist. In 2018, I finished my degree in Economics and then graduated. After completing my studies, I began working as a Social Worker in our Social Welfare department at Iris Global in Zimpeto. The main work is getting children back with families (Reintegration) and bringing in new children.

In 2019, I also started working in the girls' area as a dorm parent and we experienced a great miracle because they started to demolish and rebuild the girls' area. Today, the area has 50 girls and seven bedrooms with each room having its own bathroom. Each girl sleeps in her own bed and has a kitchen and sewing room for the girls to do the daily activities.

I decided to continue with my studies and now I am finishing a master's degree in human resource management. With this course I would like to be a manager in the future. I never, as a child, dreamed of where I would be today.

Mozambique has progressed greatly over the past 20 years, with more opportunity for education (particularly for girls), encouragement for further study and a better Social Welfare system.

I just thank God that He never left me alone. He has always been by my side taking care of me and my broken heart. He has cared for my biological family, and I now have a wonderful relationship with each of them. I no longer have my father (he passed away last year in August), but I am happy that I was able to forgive him.

I often think about everything I have experienced: the difficulties as a child and all the things I have learned and done, that now have been left behind. At these moments, I am overwhelmed with God's faithfulness and for the many people who have helped me get where I am today.

I pray that, in years to come, I will remember more of life's experiences - both good and bad - as these will serve for me to grow spiritually and strengthen my life.

Right now, I am thankful to God for everything that I have, and my hope is I will continue to grow and be a wonderful example in my family and local community. I am a very happy and fulfilled person because of the help of God and the people of Iris Global Zimpeto that He put in my path. I can realize my dream: to study and to have Jesus as Lord of my life. I have a wonderful family. For all of this I am grateful to God.

My life has not been a "bed of roses" as I have faced many difficulties in life. I am made of flesh and blood, and I have feelings. I live with my emotions alive, and above all I have a good heart. So, what can be done about the pain and that each one of us carries in life? After much reflection, it's easy to say that I have problems, pains, and hurts, just like so many other people. Today, I believe that nothing lasts forever and that sometimes difficult things happen in our lives. These trials are for our growth.

As John 16:33 says: "In this world you will have trouble". But the verse does not stop there – it goes on to say, "But take heart! I have overcome the world."

I want to live my life in peace and not just to please others. Therefore, I live life with Jesus at the centre, in my own way. Accepting myself has lessened the reality of life's pain. My struggles lead me to enjoy the good times and learn from life. Live life while you can to the fullest, for one of these days the curtain will close!!

So I leave this message to you:

In time of war, never stop praying. Do not look at how far your goals may be or listen to people who did not have the strength to fight for a goal, and who do not believe that it is possible to achieve everything they once dreamed of. Be courageous. Say "I CAN" even before you start, and after you start do not stop for anything in this world.

Write a word each day, and at the end a book will be written, the book of your life. On the cover will be written I WON!

Even when we feel alone and lost, Jesus is with us, showing us the right direction to go and the best way. (Jesus is the Way!) We are victorious people for the simple fact that we are alive and have gained a new opportunity every day to conquer something new and to seek to be better in every way.

I am so thankful for all the victories I have ever achieved in my life, from the hardest to the simplest. With each victory I feel more alive, more blessed, more loved and even more protected. With each victory I become more confident that the next battles will also be won. Fear is no longer an obstacle, and knowing God leaves me very grateful! It wasn't easy, but it was worth it.

I thank my God, for another victory achieved!

In Philippians 3:12-13 the Bible says: "Not that I have already obtained all of this, or have already arrived at my goal, but I press on to take hold of that for which Christ Jesus took hold of me. Brothers and sisters, I do not consider myself yet to have taken hold of it. But one thing I do: Forgetting what is behind and straining toward what is ahead, I press on toward the goal to win the prize for which God has called me heavenward in Christ Jesus."

It is with great pleasure that I thank God for all that I have achieved to date.

I acknowledge my effort and recognise my failures because I know none of them were big enough to make me give up. On the contrary, my mistakes have helped me grow.

Thank you so much, my God, for all the good you have done in my life. For those things which have not brought me happiness remind me that YOU overcame on the cross and you are the prize.

I want to thank everyone who directly or indirectly helped me on this journey. There were many challenges to be faced.

I also thank my family for always being by my side to support me in good times and bad. Thanks...

With a lot of love.

Hilda Francisco

Stories of Hope | 163

Hilda and her 2 children

University graduation

CHAPTER 13

Jimia Guite

MY NAME IS Jimia Guite. I am 25 years old and I have a sister (Nucha Guite) and a brother (Frenk Guite).

I was born in September 1999. We had a beautiful family. Three months later, in December, my father died. I was just a baby and I didn't know anything about it. I am sure that it was a terrible Christmas for my family. Four years later, while my family was trying to recover, my mother died. That is when my life, and that of my siblings, became chaotic.

My father had two families. When my mother died, my aunt took care of us. Then, we were evicted, because my stepmother (my father's other wife) claimed that the house belonged to her. We had nowhere to live because the aunt who took care of us did not have a house of her own. We went to live together with my grandmother.

My grandmother was very, very poor. We depended on her just to survive. Months later she heard about a place that helped children with different difficulties, and she took us there. That place is Íris Global Zimpeto. I arrived with my brother and sister, and I remember that I cried a lot because my sister and I did not get to sleep in the same room, because we were not the same age!

But they welcomed us and we grew up there. Meanwhile, my brother was transferred to another centre, Iris Global Machava, where he grew up. When my sister turned 15, she went to live with a pastor (Nico and his wife Laurinda) who had a big heart for helping others. I continued studying and growing there on the Zimpeto base.

Something very beautiful happened to me there: I accepted Jesus as my Lord and Saviour and I was baptised.

When I was in the 11th grade, I was reintegrated (reunited with family) and went to live in the house of my aunt who had taken care of us when I was little. I continued to study, and finished high school!

It was not easy moving from one house to another, but God made me realize that no matter the circumstances, He will always be with me!

My family could not afford to support my studies. I had no idea what was coming. I was told that Iris Global would pay for my college education. It was one of the best miracles of my life. I am at the end of this academic journey and have been studying Accounting and Auditing at the University of São Tomas in Mozambique.

These four years have not been easy for me. I had to work hard to get good grades and good results. In 2020, during the COVID-19 era, my uncle, who is our provider at home, lost his job. I was not working because of the pandemic. It was difficult to eat because we had no money coming in to the house. That time was horrible.

Sometimes, I would go out to a soccer field near my house just to be able to scream a little because we didn't know who to ask for help. The people we thought would help us didn't.

All we had was God.

I continued studying, but because of the pandemic, it was on Zoom. Sometimes, I could not attend classes because I did not have the money to pay for the internet. Yet Jesus had not abandoned us, and we survived that storm.

Last year, 2023, was a very difficult year for me. I think God was testing me because nothing I wanted was working out. I wanted to finish my final project, but I couldn't because someone stole my belongings, which contained the computer that I had been working on. I almost got kidnapped, and I was very angry with God because it seemed like He had forgotten about me. I started to close my heart to God, claiming that it was His fault that everything was going wrong. I spent a few months just blaming God. I hadn't realised that everything has a purpose.

I kept talking to Him, even though I felt like He was not listening to me and His presence was no longer noticeable. I kept seeking Him, because the Word says that even in silence, the Lord is working!

Now I am working and finishing my final project. In these last few years, God has placed missions on my heart, and other dreams that seem impossible to achieve. Yet I know that what seems impossible in the eyes of men is possible in His eyes, because nothing is impossible for God!

I love the children in Zimpeto and I have been helping in one of the dormitories - mostly with 10 to 12 year old boys.

I am also overseeing the Hospitality area, which receives several hundred visitors a year, from all over the world.

So, I am hoping to be able to achieve the dreams that God has placed in my heart.

I always remember this verse: "For I know the plans I have for you," declares the Lord, "plans to prosper you and not to harm you, plans to give you hope and a future." (Jeremiah 29:11)

Jimia as a child

Jimia with friends Hilda and Aniceta

CHAPTER 14

Joaneta Zitha

My name is Joaneta Agostinho Zitha and I was born on 13 November 1998.

I came to Iris Ministries (now Iris Global) with my brother Luís in the year 2000. He was six months old and I was one year and 6 months old. Luís and I joined Iris Ministries primarily because I lost my biological mother. My biological father was unable to take care of us. I also had many difficulties walking. I don't have any memories before I came to Iris but I am told that both my brother and I had tuberculosis which was treated when I came into the Iris centre. My growth was also stunted. I used to think about my mother, and I would miss her sometimes. However, I knew she didn't have good conditions to live well. I learned to pray and be thankful for the things we had here. I also learned not to have a baby as young as my mother was.

Luís and I lived in the baby house. There I was looked after with much love and affection from all the tias (carers) who worked at that time. My brother and I were among the children chosen and privileged to be cared for by Papa Steve and Mana Ros in their house in 2002. During a chicken pox outbreak, the sickest and most vulnerable babies were removed from the baby house. Papa Steve and Mana Ros took 10 children into their home. When the chicken pox passed we stayed there. We lived there until we left the base as adolescents.

Luís is my brother and because we were together, I didn't feel so lonely. I felt like I also had the responsibility to care for and protect him. Luís suffers from asthma so sometimes I felt frightened he might die from asthma. I love him very much. Even when he is far away, I still have him in my heart. I pray for him and pray he won't forget about me his sister and that he will follow his dreams and that they will come true. I know if he is happy, I will be happy.

The first time I remember meeting my maternal grandmother was when I was about 11 years old. The family all came to meet Luís and I, including my aunties and uncles.

It made me happy to know my biological family and to learn a bit about my mother. Apparently, she died when she was 16 years old which means she was very young when she was pregnant with me. My father was only a few years older than her. When my mother died my grandmother gave Luís and I to my father. However he could not care for us, and his family arranged to bring us to the Iris Ministries centre in Zimpeto. At this time my maternal grandmother did not know where we were. She looked around for quite a long time till she found us at the centre.

When we were little Papa Steve and Mana Ros spoke to us in English so we could learn. We often went on outings to the city for our birthdays or to the swimming pool. We studied in a good school in the city. Most of all, we learned about Jesus and to love one another. Papa Steve and Mana Ros always demonstrated their love for us and for Jesus as their Lord and Saviour.

Since then, many good and bad things have happened, but I never gave up on my dreams.

For me living in the centre was a privilege because I was cared for and had the opportunity to go to school and to go to other places like the pool, restaurants, museums, and the the cinema. I got to see life outside. I met many people from other parts of the world who came to bless us like Pastor Kathy from Australia. We always had food and special presents on June the 1st (which is Children's Day) and Christmas.

Sometimes we had so much fun with the tias and our other brothers at the pool. I remember we ate lasagne, pizza and other good food. We learned how to save our money although I didn't really save well.

I attended school on the centre and have finished Grade 12.

I got married in the Zimpeto church to my husband Inacio in 2018, and we have two children: a girl who is now (in 2024) seven years old and attending 2nd class at the Iris Global school, and a two-year-old boy.

After our wedding, the Ministry gave us one of their houses to live in close to the centre. This house has blessed me and my family. In 2021, I was given a job on the centre helping the girls in the girls' area.

I was helped by others, and I thank God for life, and for Him working miracles in my life. My family gives me great joy. If it were not for Jesus, I would not be alive today. God healed me and gave me health, and a voice which I use to glorify Him in the church, where I am part of the praise and worship group. I praise God wherever I go.

I am grateful for the lives of Papa Steve and Mana Ros for all the support they have given me since I was little until today. They never gave up on me.

In the future, I would like to train as a Nurse or a Doctor. Mana Ros is a nurse and is my inspiration.

Thank you, Heidi and Rolland Baker for listening to God's voice and for thinking about children in need in this country. May God continue to bless your lives richly and abundantly.

Thank you Iris Global Zimpeto!

Joaneta growing up

With husband Inacio and children

Stories of Hope | 173

Joaneta with Papa Steve & Mana Ros

With her grandmother Madelina

CHAPTER 15

João Vasco Novela

MY NAME IS João Vasco Novela. I come from a very poor background. I have two older brothers.

One day my father was away with work. When he returned, they told him, "Your wife has had a baby." He asked them, "What sort of baby is it?" They said it was a boy. He replied, "Another boy?" He spat and left. In his mind and his heart, he really wanted a girl, so the fact that I was born a boy was not something that pleased him. He decided to leave the house and left us all alone.

We lived in a rented house, and when he left, my mother could not afford the rent. So, we had to leave that house, and we began to live in many different houses. My mother had to do lots of housekeeping jobs to find somewhere to put us, and to get a little bit of bread to feed us. It was not easy. She also had problems with alcohol. That problem grew until her drinking was out of control. It made our life very, very tough, to the point where my brother decided to go out and try to find a job selling plastic, to be able to feed us.

By the grace of God, I went on growing, but it got tougher and tougher. My brother had an idea: find an orphanage where they could look after me, and where I would have access to school. He found out about Iris Ministries, and the whole family decided that they wanted to take me there. So, they did take me there, and when we arrived, I was introduced to Mama Aida by other boys. They said this was my new home. Well, it was a beautiful place: so many people! But it did not work for me. I had just experienced hunger and now I was coming to a season of experiencing something else: hatred and rejection. To me, the fact that they would take me away from home and put me in some place where there were 300 strangers, was not love. Three hundred other kids, most of them coming from the streets. I could not understand. I could not feel safe there.

Mama Aida welcomed me. She gave me my first shower, after months without a shower, and she said to me, "Welcome home! You are dearly loved!" But still there was a pounding in my little head: I could not understand. I just wanted to escape from that place. I wanted to go home, although I did not know the way. This began to raise an angry spirit in me. I felt so rejected. Although there were a lot of people around me trying to be nice to me, trying to speak nice words to me, trying to love me, it never worked. So, that just made me grow with anger in my heart, and due to this anger, I just wanted to hurt everyone. I was hurting inside, and I wanted to hurt everyone around me. So, whenever a child tried to approach me, I wanted to take whatever thing I could find nearby – a rock or a stick – and just wanted to beat them up. I wanted them to feel what I was feeling inside my heart. I was hurting, I was broken, I was lonely.

At Zimpeto, we had to go to church three or four times a week. I had never been to church before. They had instruments there, and everyone was praising, everyone was worshipping, everyone was dancing. They were laughing, full of joy. I could not understand a thing. I was lost in that place. I began to say to myself, "What's happening with these people? Why are they laughing? Why are they so joyful? I live in this very same place, but I don't experience that joy." All the kids were happy, running around, while I would find a corner and sit down, and just watch them. I literally said to myself, "These must be the craziest people ever on this planet." They really were. They were crazy for Jesus, crazy for the Holy Spirit, but I could not understand. So, I would just find my corner every time I went to church and watch everybody. Everybody could see that I was broken and lonely, even though the Holy Spirit and many friendly people were there.

One day, Pastor José approached me. He sat down with me and said, "Are you OK?" I said I was fine. He said, "Why aren't you dancing?" I replied, "I don't want to dance. I'm good the way I am." One Sunday went by, another Thursday went by, and I felt like Pastor José had his eyes on me, and he would not leave me alone. He kept coming over to ask me, "Don't you want to dance? Don't you want to rejoice?" Then he took my hand and led me up to where they were dancing. He began to dance. I danced with him, but just to make him leave me alone. I was not engaging. I could not find myself in that environment.

Time went by. Back then we used to have a lot of visitors, who usually came for two to three weeks. All these visitors could see that I was hurting, I was broken, and I was lonely. They tried to invite me in. They tried to talk to me and gave me nice words, but it never worked. I could not understand a word they were saying. I could not speak English, so it just made things worse. They tried to love on me, but I was so closed and locked up. I could not receive love, and I couldn't give love.

There was a team from California. Every day, they came to me. They took me for a walk and tried to say all these nice words to me, but I still could not understand a thing. They called some boys to come and translate for me. They insisted that I should get involved with other kids, that I should play, and receive this "joy", and they kept speaking about Jesus to me. I got so sick and tired of this, to the point where I made the best mistake ever: I challenged God. I was only eight years old, but I said, "God, if you exist, please help me to understand what these white people are trying to say to me." And that is when I began to open a path for the Holy Spirit to work within me.

After a week I could understand a little bit. A month later I could hold a conversation. I thought, "Wow! How can this be possible?" It had taken me a couple of months just to learn Portuguese, my second language, at school. English was coming faster than Portuguese. I began to try to speak English to the visitors, and some of them gave me a dictionary. Back then I could not read - that was another problem. I kept that dictionary, but I learned just from speaking to them.

One day, a few months later, I heard that Charles, the translator in church, was sick. I remember Papa Steve coming to me, saying, "João, could you translate for us this Thursday? We have many visitors, and the translator is not well." I remember I did not have a moment's hesitation. I replied straightaway, and said, "No. I don't speak English. I can't translate." Papa Steve said, "The little English you speak will help us tonight." I said, "There's no way I'm doing that." So, Papa Steve asked me to go to my dorm and pray, and then to come and talk to him when the siren went off for us all to go to church. I said I would do that, though deep in my heart I was still saying, "NO!" I chose to respect him. I went to my room, and I began to pray. I do not know if the Holy Spirit was absent, because I came out of that room, still with a big "NO! I am not translating tonight!"

The siren went off. It was time to go to church. I went there, and I tried to hide. Papa Steve was searching or me everywhere. He found me and said: "Are you ready?" I gave him another big "NO!" The church service started and, suddenly, Papa Steve grabbed the mic and called me up. Oh no! I wanted a big pit to open so I could hide myself. I wanted to disappear. But, once again, I chose to respect him. I walked up. He handed me the mic and told me that he was going to speak in Portuguese, but that these people would not understand Portuguese. He said, "Just say anything in English! They will be excited!" So, Papa Steve began to speak in Portuguese, and I translated it to English. Sometimes he switched from Portuguese to English, and there I was, still translating. I just opened my mouth and found words flowing out. I did not even understand what I was saying, but, praise God, the people understood.

After the church service Papa Steve said, "Well done!", and everyone came running to embrace me, telling me I had done a great job. I still did not know what had happened or what I had said. I spent two days praying in my room. After every meal I would be back there. I would not go out. I was just sitting in my room saying: "God, thank you. From now on I want to use this gift in your Kingdom. I want to use it for you." Since that day, I have been using my gift of the English language to translate for the Kingdom in church services and conferences. This is still what I do today.

So, it was beautiful, but I still had a problem. I could not deal with myself, with the anger and hatred I felt in my heart. This was hindering my life. One day I decided I needed to forgive my father. I felt hatred for him and anger too. I felt everything went wrong because he left me. When I heard that he left me when I was born just because I was yet another boy, that hurt me even more. I did not choose to be born a boy. I did not even choose to be born. It was all God's plan. His design.

I tried to forgive my father in my own strength. I tried and prayed, but it was not working. The anger was too deep. So, I said, "Lord, help me."

I remember God replying, "João, forgiving your father is not your responsibility." He said, "You must forgive yourself for choosing to hold anger against him. Your father is my son. Your father is not your responsibility. Let me deal with him." I said, "Lord, it hurts. What he did was not right." He replied, "Yes, but it's not your mission to stand in judgement. I love him. I love him more than you can understand." I said, "God, how? How can that be? How can you love him when he rejected me and left us to go through so much suffering?" He said, "Your father is my son. I love him dearly. Your mission is to forgive yourself. I have him and I will keep him accountable. Let go and gain your freedom."

I fell face down and I said I couldn't. I could not forgive him. I did not know how to. And God said, "That's what I needed to hear. I know you can forgive, but I also know you don't know **how** to forgive him. So, would you let me in? Stop serving me empty. Stop serving me wounded. Stop trying to love me empty. Stop trying to love me wounded. Would you walk with me on this journey of forgiveness? We are talking about **your** life. Stop worrying about other people. Worry about **your** life right now. I want to deal with you João. I want to love you. I want to forgive you. Stop trying to free other people, while you're still in prison."

So, I began to walk with the Lord in this mission of forgiveness. Let me tell you, it is very easy when you must deal with someone else's problems, but dealing with yourself is the toughest. I had to be honest with myself – bring everything out that was so filthy and bad. Dealing with it was not an easy journey. But I went on that journey, step by step, day by day.

At some stage I began to feel peace deep inside my heart and soul. I had finally been released from the prison of bitterness against my own father. I understood that he also deserved to be forgiven and loved. (Here I was, fighting to forgive someone whose face I did not even know!) All this really helped me to understand God as God the Father. I had always struggled with this. I had received Him as the Almighty, but not as a loving Father, because I had the wrong image of a father. For so many years I never even wanted to have a father, or to become a father. I did not have the best image of what a mother was, but it was a thousand times better than my image of a father. God helped me to restore this image and to understand its importance.

When I went to Iris, my brothers went to South Africa to try to find a better life out there. Since the day when we separated, we have not seen each other. I really pray that, one day, we can meet. I pray for that day of encounter with my brothers and my father, where – on Earth or in Heaven – I meet them and tell them I am alive. I am alive because of Jesus! If they have not walked the journey of forgiveness, I want to help them. I want them to walk in freedom and love. I want to tell them I love them.

So, this journey of forgiveness helped me as I grew up at Iris. It helped me to be a good brother to the children who came from the streets and to the orphaned kids. As Mama Aida always preached, I was no longer an orphan. I had a Daddy. I had a Papa, and my Daddy was God, who loved me every day and night. He always cared about me. As I continued to grow up, going to church, doing good things and serving God, I asked Him, "How can I repay you? How can I repay you for your kindness? How can I repay you for your love?"

And I found out there would never be enough words that I could use to thank God. The only way that I could thank Him would be by doing the same to others. I had to stop for others, as somebody had stopped for me. I had to love unconditionally as someone had loved me unconditionally. I had to forgive others as God had forgiven me.

So here I am now. I have started a project where we train young people to have practical skills. We train them in carpentry, welding, sewing, and working with electricity. We are a training centre. This was possible because God stopped for me. Mama Aida stopped for me. Papa Steve stopped for me. Mana Ros stopped for me. These people sowed a seed of love in my life. Here I am today trying to continue their great example.

I want to take this chance to say to Papa Steve and Mana Ros: thank you very, very much for never giving up, and for showing love and kindness beyond measure to me. I am the man I am today because you stopped for me, because you loved me.

Please never stop praying for me. My heart's desire is to give something back - to continue to run the race, and help my fellow brothers learn skills, so they can provide for their families; so, they can give back to the nation and contribute to the growth of Mozambique.

Mama Aida, Papa Rolland, Papa Steve, Mana Ros: Mozambique would not be the same without your love. This nation will forever be thankful to you. Keep on! I know sometimes it feels like a drop in the ocean. It feels like it does not make a difference, but you are making a mega difference in this nation.

We study because of you. We train people because of you. I am at university because you stopped for me. I am learning International Relations and International Law: I want to be able to defend others and make Mozambique a better place. It is all because you prayed night and day for God to touch lives, to provide for us, to give access to school and access to our own homes.

Yesterday I was a child and today I am a man. Today I am a father. Today I am married. I can be an example, a witness to others: with God, everything is possible. I encourage my fellow brothers: do not give up. There is still hope unless you give up. There is still a better tomorrow. I thank God, above all, for the lives of all the people around the world who donate, and who pray for the people of Mozambique. I see God in Heaven, standing with His arms open and with a crown of glory waiting for all the wonderful people who are supporting ministries all over the world. God is saying, "Well done, my faithful servants". There is a crown for whoever involves themselves with a ministry that helps to better the lives of young people, better the lives of people all over the world. You are dearly loved by God for being His hands and feet. I will forever thank God for you.

I love you. Be blessed.

João and family

João with Pastor Luís Cabral

CHAPTER 16

Mónica Machel

MY NAME IS Mónica Machel. I am 24 years old, and I was born in Maputo in the district of Kamubuakwana.

My story began when my parents got married, and had me and my brothers: a total of three children. We were a very happy and harmonious family but then the hardest phase of my life began in 2003, when I was three years old. My mother became mentally ill, which took her away from me, her family and her friends.

My life, and that of my family became very difficult, and there were many challenging days. I remember that we had to live on the streets with our mother. The streets became our home. In order to survive, she begged and accepted food from strangers. As time went on, my mother faced the harsh reality of life on the streets with us. There was not enough food, and the nights were cold and scary. I remember that we even slept in the woods because she felt it was the best way to snuggle up together safely.

Although she had mental health problems, she never allowed it to erase the hope in our eyes. Although she faced daily challenges, she strived to do her best for us. Even though she was sick, my mother never forgot her children, no matter what state she was in.

Our maternal grandmother was always a strong woman. Her life was not easy, because of her daughter's mental health problems, and she worried about how to make things better. She tried to take care of us, but my mother came after us and took us back to live on the streets, which was not healthy for us as children.

Our grandmother showed persistence and unconditional love. In 2004, through a lot of research, she learned of a centre: a place that offered shelter and support to people who were in vulnerable situations. This was how me and my brother Silavio Pedro were welcomed into the Zimpeto Centre. (We didn't know where our other brother was, but he was living with our aunt.)

I remember being welcomed unreservedly by the team at Zimpeto. First I lived in the Baby House, which is for children aged from birth to four years old. There, I made lasting friendships.

In 2006 I was transferred to the girls' dormitory. I learned many things there and met incredible friends (Marta and Hilda). I also met missionaries (Anna, Esther, Fiona, Natasha, Rachel and Tracey) who had a positive impact on my life and provided great affection to me on my journey.

During this time, I did not see my mother at all, but our grandmother never stopped visiting us. Other family members were also there to support us. Our grandmother did her best to take care of our mother, whose mental illness was becoming overwhelming. In 2007, things got worse for my grandmother: she faced the toughest challenge of losing two of her daughters - my aunts - to illness. (Later, in 2014, my mother and her brother also died from illnesses. This was very painful for me because I had not seen my mother since 2004. My grandmother, who had six children, now only had two daughters left).

Meanwhile, in 2007 I started studying in first grade, where I met Professora Rosa, who is no longer with us. She taught me to read and write well. There were several teachers who imparted good knowledge to me, but she was one of the first and most impactful sources of inspiration, giving me confidence and motivation at school.

After that, I passed through the grades without failing. There is so much more I could say, but I will just mention the most important parts of my student journey. In 2014, I was named one of the best students in the school due to my effort, participation, dedication and commitment. In 2017, I studied Art, and won first place with a drawing, which was named one of the best drawings in the school. In 2018 I was elected as the best student from Iris Global.

Since then, I have gained many new opportunities:

In 2017, I joined the worship group at the Partners in Harvest Church, where I serve as a member to this day.

In 2018, I joined the Sunday School as a teacher, where we teach children about God's commandments, and how to seek first the Kingdom of God and His righteousness, in order to find true peace, purpose and fulfilment in our daily lives.

In 2018, I had the experience of being helped to return to live with my grandmother. I now live with her and my brother, and it has been a very pleasant experience.

In 2019, thanks to Papa Steve, Mana Ros, and other leaders - who encouraged and championed my academic career - I had the opportunity to pursue – and achieve - a degree in Civil Engineering.

I am currently a student at Wutivi University. I am now studying Engineering, Architecture and Physical Planning, and have completed four years of study. I am preparing my Dissertation, to graduate soon.

I have already applied some of the knowledge acquired through my academic career. For example, I have participated in several internships, including one at a construction site at Wutivi University (running a Mechanical Engineering laboratory at the institution). I am motivated to do my best in every challenge that comes my way.

My favorite verses from the Bible are Ephesians 6:11-12, which teach us to put on the full armour of God, so that we can stand against the schemes of the devil. These verses also teach us that our struggle is "not against flesh and blood but against the rulers, against the authorities, against the powers of this dark world, and against the spiritual forces of evil in the heavenly realms."

Mónica as a child

Stories of Hope | 189

Mónica at work (third from left)

Aniceta and Mónica

CHAPTER 17

Nhelety Mandlate

Hello! My name is Nhelety Francisco Mandlate. I am 18 years old and I am studying my first year of Civil Engineering at university.

My story began in 2011, when I joined the Zimpeto base of Iris Ministries at the age of five. Before that, I lived in the Nursery at the Primeiro de Maio orphanage, but I do not have many memories of how I got there, as I was too little to understand the situation. What I do know is that those early years were marked by many changes and challenges that shaped my character from an early age.

Growing up at Zimpeto was a profoundly transformative experience. It was there that I met God and began to develop a deep, personal relationship with Him. I found a welcoming community that supported and guided me through every step of my growth. I discovered my talents and abilities, and from an early age I strove to be a good student and a person of integrity, even though I made natural childhood mistakes. The educators (child carers in the dormitories) gave me excellent training, not only academically, but also morally and spiritually. I studied there until the 10th grade, learning important values that I carry with me to this day, such as honesty, responsibility, and love for others.

All this time, in my daily prayers, I asked God to bless me with a family. This was a deep desire in my heart, and I knew it would only come true at the right time. Therefore, I always tried to respect the process and trust in God's plan for my life. Then, in November 2021, I received news which completely changed my life: I had the unique opportunity to join a family. That moment was a true miracle for me, something I will never forget.

Today, thank God, I am part of a family that welcomed me with open arms as a beloved member. This experience has been a great blessing in my life. I am very happy and immensely grateful for everything that happened. I continue studying with dedication at college and following my dreams, knowing that God has always been and will be by my side, guiding my steps. The support of my new family has been crucial for me to fully dedicate myself to my studies and achieve my goals.

My gratitude to Iris Global is eternal. It was there that I found the solid foundation that sustains me to this day, both in my studies and in my personal life. The ministry provided me not only with education, but also with values and an unshakeable faith in God. Everything I am and everything I still hope to be, I owe to the love and care I received during all these years at Zimpeto.

As I navigate my way through college, I am reminded daily of the lessons and blessings I have received. I am determined to repay all that love and support by helping others and continuing to live by the principles I have learned. I know that, with God by my side, I can face any challenge and achieve any dream. And it is with this spirit of gratitude and faith that I face the future, ready for everything that is to come.

Stories of Hope | 193

Nhelety

CHAPTER 18

Rabia Senda

MY NAME IS Rabia Rene Emílio Ojomodave Senda, daughter of Rene Emílio Ojomodave and Maria Armando Mandlate. The surname Senda comes from my husband, César Augusto Senda.

I was born on 19 April 1981, in Chibuto in the province of Gaza, and grew up in the city of Maputo. I started studying at Escola Primária do Alto Maé, in 1987.

I lost my mother when I was seven years old. I had five brothers and we were taken by our maternal grandparents back to Chibuto to live with them during the 16 year Civil war. Our grandparents claimed that my father had not paid an appropriate dowry for my mother, and therefore we would have to pay for her dowry. It was a very sad and difficult experience because we lived like helpless children. Our grandparents did not work.

After two years, we heard that my father had died from sickness. We were unable to attend our father's funeral because of lack of finances. We began to suffer, without school, without family and without anyone to support us. In the midst of this dilemma, we fled from one place to another, and ate food from the trash, or asked/begged people to give us biscuits, so we had something to eat.

People started talking to our grandparents about us working as servants in their houses. It was then that I was chosen by a lady to come to Maputo to work in her house as a maid. I was 12 years old. In 1992, she took me from Gaza, in Chibuto, back to Maputo province.

I planned to run away, once I arrived in Maputo, to look for the house of my uncle, my late father's brother, because I wanted to continue with my studies. In fact, when I arrived in the Maputo suburb of Benfica, I ran away from the truck I was in, claiming I wanted to go to the bathroom. I managed to escape to my uncle's house, in the Malanga neighborhood of Maputo. I was welcomed by my uncle and his wife. After some time, my brothers also arrived at the house. My aunt did not like this, and sent my older brother away to live on the street. My older sister and I were then admitted to the Chihango Educational Centre in 1994.

My uncle sold the house and moved to the Laulane neighborhood. In the Chihango centre, we were forgotten. My family no longer visited us. We only returned to my uncle's new house in December, to spend the vacation there. My aunt sent my older sister away. She had to have an arranged marriage.

In January 1995, Mama Aida arrived at the centre in Chihango where I was living. She told me about the love of Jesus. She showed me the love of a mother, and my story began to change because of this amazing woman. She was a present, attentive and patient mother. I learned a lot from her. Mama Aida made me realise that I was loved, had great value, and was dear to the Lord.

I learned to depend on Jesus, because He is the way, the truth and the life. I began to cling to Jesus and my life began to change. Mama Aida told me about forgiving others and not holding on to grudges. These words helped me a lot.

At this time, I lived like a princess but, in 1997, the Mozambican government asked Mama Aida and Papa Rolland to leave Chihango. We went to live in their house in Malhangalene. There were 60 children. This time was very difficult because Mama Aida's family had very little money. We bought three pounds of cornmeal to make xima and cabbage for our meal.

One day, Mama Aida called me and said, "Daughter, I don't have money today, I don't know what we are going to eat." I was sad and silent.

Suddenly, someone called Mama Aida and said she and her family were coming to the house for lunch. I brought in a small amount of beans and rice in two small pans. Mama Aida took this food and told me to serve it onto the plates. I looked at her thinking she was starting to lose her mind. There was not enough food. After praying, Mama Aida turned to me to indicate I should begin serving, and the lady who brought the food asked, "Why didn't you tell me you had a huge family in your house?" Mama Aida did not respond and gave me the order again. I served the food. We all ate and there was food left over. This was the first miracle I saw happen in my life, and I decided to love and follow Jesus Christ that day.

We left the house in the city and went to Machava. The ministry was given a church to live in. As there were so many of us, Mama Aida and Papa Rolland rented some houses nearby, and we lived there. Later, they obtained the Machava land and, in a short time, the Zimpeto land (where the centre now exists). It was a very rewarding experience.

Mama Aida and Papa Rolland invited me to Pemba to assist in the Children's centre and with Social Welfare. I became a leader in the new Iris Ministries base in the city of Pemba. There I learned many things and this encouraged me to love other children.

I am married to César, who I met during our days in Chihango. We were maried in 1997. I have a blessed family. We have six biological children and we take care of four more children.

I returned to the city of Maputo in 2018.

I now work with widows, street children, orphans and disadvantaged children. I have a project called Fundação Agape na Rua (Foundation of Love on the Streets). The objective is to reintegrate children back into their families and, if they are unable to do so, to assist them with a basic food basket. I also enrol them in school, and purchase school supplies and uniforms. I love my project.

I learned from someone - and was touched by the Spirit of God - to do for others what someone once did for me. That someone is Mama Aida.

I should also mention that I have a very patient counsellor called Francisco (the National Administrator), whom I consider an older brother. He has helped me and encouraged me a lot to move forward. I ask God, the Almighty, to help him and bless him for everything he has done for me. Francisco, thank you for helping me with your advice. Francisco, you are very important to my life and in the life of my family.

Stories of Hope | 199

Rabia and César

Rabia, César, family and Mama Heidi

CHAPTER 19

Ramos Macamo

My name is Ramos Silvano Macamo, although all my friends call me "Ramito". I was born in Mozambique in the capital city of Maputo, in 1990.

I lived in Maputo until the age of 20, when I received a sponsorship through Iris Ministries to study in Chicago, where I completed a B.Sc. in Business Administration and Management.

From where I started to where I stand right now, it is a clear demonstration of the work of God. The book of Jeremiah gives us an illustration of the work of God whereby it illustrates him as the pot maker and we as the clay. "Like clay in the hand of the potter, so are you in my hand." (Jeremiah 18:7, paraphrased).

Certainly, God has been moulding my life from the very beginning and I am very happy to see the broken pieces of clay that he is putting together to make a beautiful vase. In doing so, God has used many people through Iris Ministries to make me the person that I am. It is my dream that, as I share this testimony, the love of God and His embrace will also help you receive the same grace to mend what is broken, and that the world will rejoice in the final work of art that God creates.

From the thousands of children involved with Iris Ministries in Mozambique, it is fair to say that there are many thousands of amazing testimonies, and mine is not an exception. For this reason, I am deeply honoured to have been asked to share my testimony.

My childhood was not dissimilar to many other children who grew up at the different bases run by Iris. Fortunately, I spent most of my early years at the base in Zimpeto in the capital city of Mozambique, the base where Steven and Ros Lazar, or as we call them "Papa Steve and Mama Ros", dedicated most of their lives to take care of orphaned, neglected, and abandoned children, loving us and teaching us to live in a family, despite our tragic beginnings.

I was born into a broken and dysfunctional family and, being the youngest of six siblings, I relied mostly on what my older brothers and sisters told me about our parents. From what I recall, at the age of four my mother took all my siblings and me to an orphanage at Chihango that was run by the communist government - the group which had been at the forefront of the Mozambican liberation movement and independence from the Portuguese colonial regime (FRELIMO party).

The war of independence lasted many years. A lot had to be done to gain independence from over 500 years of slavery to which the country had been subjected. As a result of this long struggle for independence, the country was in complete disarray. Nonetheless, the Declaration of Independence in 1975 brought about a new and fresh beginning filled with hope, but the peace did not last for very long. The Declaration of Independence paved the way for internal conflicts among various groups in Mozambique as they struggled to define what the newly formed country would look like. This period of political instability lasted for over 15 years.

The first peace accord was signed in 1992 in Berlin. This accord was fundamental for the development of the country because it paved the way for investment in the country. Moreover, what most interests me is that, after this accord, the Mozambican borders were also open for hosting missionaries in the country. To them, I am forever grateful. It is because of their presence in Mozambique that today I am the person that I am.

Even though the ceasefire agreement was reached, peace and political and economic stability remained fragile in the country. Residues of war are still visible today in many regions of the country and in the lives of many communities, which these tragic events have forever changed.

I did not experience the brutalities of war, but I was born in time to see the negative effects that the war had caused to my beloved Mozambique and my beloved brothers and sisters. Because of the war, the state of the economy since independence had been stagnant. The government had not invested in anything else other than armaments to fuel the war. Families devastated, villages and houses destroyed, children orphaned and the nation in chaos: these were the realities in the 1990's. Only in recent years is the nation seeing a sign of recovery.

Many children were victimised by the war, which took away their parents, leaving them orphaned. I was born in a place where social structure was non-existent, and family values did not prevail. My father disappeared when I was two years old. I never got to see his face, or hear his voice, nor do I remember his arms wrapped around me. The tragedy that decimated the nation is still felt today by many people and children who have survived that harshness. These children, most of whom are adults today, either developed a cold and hard heart, or died due to a lack of intervention from outside forces or even heavenly forces.

For those who are living under difficult circumstances, it is very difficult to believe the goodness of God and the beauty that He has created in this universe, because everything that they have seen and tasted is hatred, pain, and suffering. My early days were characterised by rejection, and that same hatred, pain, and suffering. Looking back as I reflect while writing this testimony, it feels like I was in a tunnel buried under the earth, cradled with deep darkness: and walking through it, it seemed as if I would never get to see the light. I am grateful to the people that God brought to my life to intervene when I needed help the most, and I pray that God will send helpers for all those in need.

As I said earlier, I was only four years old when my mother, after years of struggling to support me and my brothers on her own, decided that the best option for us to have a "normal life" would be to give us to the government-run orphanage in Chihango. Normal life in this orphanage was a far-fetched idea. The leaders and founders of Iris Ministries, Mama Aida and Papa Rolland, called this place "hell on earth." From the life we experienced in this place, I agree with their description.

Approximately a year after we had been living in this orphanage, Mama Aida and Papa Rolland arrived in Mozambique and cooperated with the local government. They invested physically, emotionally, and spiritually to provide us with a life that resembles normalcy. This normal life did not last very long: the different priorities between the missionaries and the Mozambican leaders forced them to part ways, leaving us stranded again. At that point, most of us who had tasted what a normal life could look like did not want to return to our old lives. We followed the missionaries without an idea or perspective of where that path would lead us.

Today, I can attest with all certainty that this was the second-best decision of my life, second only to my first decision - which was accepting the Lord Jesus Christ as my Lord and Saviour and inviting Him into my heart to change and transform what was left of it. From this chaos, Iris Ministries was birthed in Mozambique and thank God, I became one of the children who benefited the most.

Because of my early association with the government orphanage, I had the privilege to start my education early, because it did not have a tailored-made curriculum for children. I had to join the public school with all the other children, despite my young age. This continued until I joined the base in Zimpeto when I was already in the fourth grade.

As the years passed by and I progressed in school, it all seemed normal until, one day, I was reminded of where I had come from. I was about to register to take part in the first national examination in the fifth grade. For this exam, all the other children and me from Iris who were to take part in the exams needed to have birth certificates. However, until this point, no one had registered us.

Action was taken by the leaders of Iris and, in cooperation with the government, we were issued birth certificates. For most of us, our birth certificates were issued without family affiliation, since we did not have an adult who could attest to parenthood. This is the birth certificate I used until I completed high school. It was not until my older brothers were of age that they could testify for me to have a birth certificate bearing the names of my parents. (My birth certificate issue was revisited a few years ago when I applied for permanent residency in Germany. The German consulate asked why my birth certificate had been changed, and I explained to them the story of my early childhood.)

The Iris base in Zimpeto has been a haven to many people. I spent over 20 years of my life there. By the grace of God and the sheer obedience of many missionaries from various parts of the world who had given up pursuing careers and left behind families to take care of us, I and many other people at the base were provided with the best possible lifestyle of faith, community, and a sense of belonging to a family, which otherwise we would not have had.

In 2004, I had the privilege to represent Mozambique in a forum in Barcelona, Spain. The forum gathered children from various parts of the world to discuss the development of children's rights across the world. It was after these gatherings that the United Nations, UNICEF, and Save the Children defined guidelines and metrics to be achieved as indicators of good progress for children's rights. As I reflect on the events that preceded my selection to take part in this forum, it comes to mind that it happened this way because God was intervening on my behalf. The book of Samuel explains that: " He raises the poor from the dust and lifts the needy from the ash heap; he seats them with princes and has them inherit a throne of honour." (1 Samuel 2:8). Certainly, dust and ashes are the best descriptors of my early life and there is no trace of nobility in me, so there is nothing that would qualify me other than God Himself choosing to lift me up for His glory.

This is how it came about.

In the early 2000s, the Iris base in Zimpeto had made great strides in changing the lives of many children - we were being fed, clothed, and educated. Our lives were changing for the better, and the Mozambican government was starting to take notice. Above all else, the Iris base was the place where one could find all types of children, children from broken families and with broken lives, who were being shaped and moulded into new members of the Iris family and good contributors to the Mozambican nation, but also those who would live with the perspective of the Kingdom of God.

The second president of Mozambique (Joaquim Chissano) recognised that children were the future of the nation. The Minister of Community Affairs began travelling from community to community, and meetings were held in primary schools and secondary schools to look for children to be the voice of each district. They arrived at the base in Zimpeto, where the first discussions about children's rights were to be held. Many brilliant children were selected, and I was surprised to find myself on the list.

I was also surprised when I heard most of the presentations centred around family and community, with people speaking in glowing terms about the importance of these, in creating vibrant communities and successful nations. From my experience, I had not seen a successful family. I was still learning to be part of the Iris family, which is completely different from any other ordinary family. I sensed that the perspective of children who had been torn apart from their families was completely lacking. I had no shortage of words to describe what still needed to be done for such misfortunate children.

After these debates, I was selected to be the representative of my District, and a member of the children's parliament, as an advocate of children's rights. In the following years, additional meetings were held, and this time more people were brought from across all provinces of the country. Then, at a national level, we had to give an oral presentation about the status of children's rights. From these presentations, government officials chose twelve children to represent Mozambique at the forum in Spain.

I had no confidence in myself whatsoever, because I was debating with the brightest kids who came from influential families and attended better schools than the average Mozambican. However, I was confident of one thing: I had a very different story to tell compared to many other participants. After the children's parliament session concluded, we were all invited to the Mozambican president's house, "Palacio da Ponta Vermelha", for a dinner reception. This was my first introduction to a fancy dinner, and my lack of class was evident. Nevertheless, the good news came a few weeks later: I was surprised and overjoyed to have been chosen to represent Mozambique in Spain. This was undoubtedly God selecting me: one of the world's outcasts, unwanted - and seating me with the most esteemed members of society.

Papa Steve and Mana Ros provided me with a suitcase with most of the things that I needed for my trip and, most importantly a disposable camera. My time in Barcelona was surreal. It gave me a taste of life that I had never thought existed, given the contrast between my upbringing and living situation and those of developed nations.

The forum lasted for two weeks, and then we had to return. It was an experience that I remember fondly until this day. I had the privilege to sit with many other children who were chosen to represent their countries, most of whom held a higher social class status than mine, had better manners than me, were better educated than me, and deserved to be part of this event, yet there I was by the Grace of God. I also had a chance to meet many important people, even though I did not know who they were. For example, after my return, Mana Laura – an American missionary at Zimpeto - was looking at my photos from Spain, and she saw Angelina Jolie. She was surprised, and she asked me if I knew who she was. I did not. I only remembered that she was one of the ladies who came to give a speech and spent the afternoon with us.

To this day, I ask myself how I ended up there, and the only plausible answer is that it was by the grace of God.

After my return to Zimpeto, I progressed with my studies. With the support of Iris church partners and missionaries, I was provided with the best possible educational preparation for life, career, and ministry. Today, I can say that I have been well trained by the grace of God, and He has helped me to gain some education qualifications, which I had never dreamed of achieving. In 2022, I received my first master's degree: an M.Sc. in Financial Economics, from Otto-von-Guericke University of Magdeburg and, in 2023, I received my second master's degree, an M.Sc. in Economics, and Applied Economics, from the University of Hamburg.

Currently, I am enjoying the first years of marriage. In 2022 I married my precious wife Astrid Ingrid Macamo, whom I met in Mozambique in 2010, when she visited Zimpeto with her youth group. Together, we live in Hamburg Germany, and we are active in ministry supporting the Iris Revival Online Church, started by Pastor Surpresa, and the Dock 1 Kirche, our local community of believers in Hamburg.

It is wonderful when God gifts people with both natural and supernatural wisdom to advance His kingdom. I am very glad to be part of this movement, pulling down heaven to earth, demonstrating the love of God to others, and celebrating with all other believers as His will is done in our lives and is manifested in this world.

Aside from ministry, we are also pursuing careers. I am a financial and digital transformation consultant at Deloitte, and my wife works for the Ministry of Education and Child Care as an advisor for work and organisational psychology. We are very excited and looking forward to what God is going to do in our lives as a family and in service to His kingdom.

When we met in Mozambique, we were both very young and had different priorities. Astrid, who is very determined and disciplined, was focusing on her studies at the University of Leipzig. She already had an ambition to obtain an advanced degree in Psychology (which she later obtained in 2018). Meanwhile, I was getting ready to move to Chicago to start college. Our academic ambitions aligned perfectly, and our faith also aligned perfectly, despite being raised in different environments. Yet, we did not know what the future would hold for our relationship, because we were living on different continents. We remained in contact, and only years later - when I moved to Germany to pursue a master's degree - did we establish a relationship that culminated in marriage. We are blessed beyond measure, as together we are starting a family, and together are actively pursuing the calling that God has for our lives.

In September 2023, my wife and I were blessed with the opportunity to visit Mozambique. It was our desire to stay at the Zimpeto base where I had spent my childhood, to reconnect with the educators, Mozambican staff, and some of the children who might still be there. To my surprise, many young people, who were teenagers when I left Mozambique, had since transitioned to the Iris Ministries community in Maracuene, where they are now provided with the best possible training to equip them to embrace adult life in Mozambique. I was able to see some of the young men with whom I shared the dormitory and playground.

Our lives look completely different now, because I have been living in Germany for about five years and, prior to that, I lived in the USA for seven years.

While at Zimpeto, I had the chance to visit the Baby House and the Nursery to see how much things had changed. The Baby House looks very different compared with ten years ago: there is better infrastructure in place than I remember. Yet one theme that remains constant between then and now, is the love and dedication of the educators who are taking care of the children at the base. I was very happy to see the educators who are working in the Baby House, some of whom had known me since I was six years old, or younger. Certainly, there have been many children coming into their hands as babies, infants, and children, and these educators have poured out their lives to nurture and raise them.

Besides the Baby House, the primary and secondary schools are the most visible features of the Iris base in Zimpeto. During the day, the base is filled with students attending classes, numbering from 1000 to 3000 students. The school infrastructure has significantly improved in comparison to the years I was attending primary school. We did not have proper classroom buildings: I studied under a mango tree, where I completed my fourth and fifth grades. Today, children have the luxury of well-insulated classrooms, with basic teaching materials that meet the Mozambican standard.

Iris Ministries has invested and continues to invest in the physical development of the children and community, but also in the spiritual development of the children and all those who are part of the ministry. This is a feature that remains visible today and is very important.

On my visit to Mozambique, I was happy to see that most of the ministries that were in place in the early 2000s are still running now. I used to be actively involved in evangelistic ministries, including weekend outreaches and Hospital Ministry. I was very happy to see that these ministry outreaches are still active and thriving, and that the churches that have been built because of this evangelism are also thriving.

Overall, my last visit to Mozambique was very enriching. It reminded me of the childhood that I had. Although I did not choose it for myself, it was a place where God stepped in and changed my life forever.

I am eternally grateful to all the churches, ministries, and missionaries who have tirelessly contributed to my development, and for the development of all the children at Iris Ministries: first and foremost, at the base in Zimpeto but also in many other locations. I am certain that there are many other life testimonies of radical change, and mine is just one simple story.

Ramito with Mama Aida, as a child

Ramito with his wife Astrid

As a youth in Zimpeto, with Mama Aida

CHAPTER 20

Silavio Pedro

MY NAME IS Silavio Pedro and I was born in Maputo, Mozambique, on 27 June 1998.

From a very early age, my life and that of my family were marked by difficulties. I grew up alongside my mother, my brother and my sister, but our life together was greatly impacted by the deterioration of my mother's mental health. Her condition profoundly affected our quality of life.

We lived predominantly from subsistence farming. My mother had a small patch of land where we grew different products. This land was located a considerable distance from home, and it was there that we spent most of our time. Work on the land was arduous and required a lot of physical effort. Every day, after work, we went out to the local market at Zimpeto to sell what we had grown. Despite our hard work, sales were often meagre, leaving us to face frequent periods of hunger.

The precarious financial situation and the constant need for work prevented me from attending school. I was not allowed to go there, because my mother needed our help, both on the farm and selling at the market. We walked through many markets in Maputo, from dawn to dusk, always on foot. The pain in my feet, even as a child, when walking long distances was intense and constant.

I have not mentioned my father until now because his presence in my life was practically non-existent. I grew up without a father figure, and the little information I have about him is vague and sparse. His absence was an additional challenge in our already complicated lives.

Refuge at Iris Ministries

The situation worsened significantly when my mother was forcibly admitted to Infulene Psychiatric Hospital. The worsening of her condition had led my maternal grandmother and her children to make the difficult decision to hospitalise her, for her own safety and well-being. Without my mother, the responsibility of taking care of us fell to our grandmother, who faced an immense challenge. The rest of the family was afraid, due to my mother's past aggressive behaviour, and were reluctant to help.

During the time we were in my grandmother's care, she tried to do her best for us, including intending to enroll us in school. However, the situation took an unexpected turn when my mother, in an act of desperation, managed to leave the hospital and reported our grandmother to the police, falsely claiming that she had kidnapped us to sell us. This led to my grandmother being arrested for three days. The intervention of neighbours, who were concerned about my mother's deteriorating mental state, was crucial in getting her released.

After this traumatic episode, my mother banned any visits to our grandmother. Despite my grandmother's efforts to place us in a shelter for disadvantaged children, my mother believed that our grandmother intended to sell us out and refused to let us go there.

In 2004, my grandmother and the neighbours carefully planned a solution. During a trip to the local market, my older brother - who already had a clearer idea of the situation – led. My sister Mónica and I stayed with our mother. That night, my grandmother paid a drunk man to distract my mother while someone else took us away. Mónica and I were taken from our home in an operation that felt like a kidnapping to me, and I screamed desperately. However, upon being handed over to my grandmother, I managed to calm down. My mother was in despair, believing that we were being kidnapped. My grandmother took us to a friend's house so we could spend the night safely. The next day, we were taken to Iris Ministries. My grandmother's initial plan was to take all three of us to Iris Ministries but, in the end, only Mónica and I went, while my brother grew up under the care of my aunt.

Once we were safely there, my grandmother explained the new situation to our mother, which brought some relief to me. However, I did not have the opportunity to see her again after that night in 2004, and she passed away in 2014, due to illness.

New Life at Iris Ministries

Arriving at Iris Ministries in 2004, was a transformative and totally new experience for me. When I first entered the ministry premises, I was greeted by a huge variety of children, of different ages and backgrounds. I was especially excited to realise that there were other children in my age group, which made me feel a little more at ease amidst so much new stuff.

Adapting to the new routine was relatively smooth. Mónica, my little sister, was assigned to the Baby House, as she was only four years old at the time. I was directed to Dorm five, where six-year-old children lived. Mana Katy, the missionary responsible for the dorm, welcomed me warmly with a simple but striking snack - bread with peanut butter. This was one of the first times

I had tried something so different from what I was used to, and the unusual flavour of bread with peanut butter was etched in my memory.

One of the most significant changes was starting to attend school for the first time. Initially, the experience was challenging, and the school environment was very different from what I knew. However, over time, I managed to adapt better. In second grade, I returned with renewed determination and was surprisingly voted the best student in the class. This recognition motivated me to continue studying hard and, from then on, I was often among the best students.

During my studies, I had the opportunity to learn about life, explore different countries and cultures and, most of all, meet Jesus, who became an essential part of my journey.

At Iris Ministries, I developed a great passion for football and cinema, activities that became an important part of my life. Another discovery that made a big impression on me was being able to eat three meals a day, something that was almost impossible in my previous life. It was a revelation of how food security can transform everyday life. Furthermore, I learned that people from different backgrounds and cultures can come together and form a true family. The Children's Day and Christmas celebrations were moments of intense joy and collective celebration, which were very different from the experiences I had had before. The affection and dedication of the missionaries and educators were fundamental to my development and adaptation, and these moments of warmth, care and support are remembered with great appreciation.

Reflections on Adolescence

During my adolescence at Iris Ministries, my life underwent a profound and significant transformation. I learned about life, about myself and, above all, about God, the Creator of all things. The discipleship activities promoted by the missionaries played a fundamental role in this growth process. They were much more than just classes: they were moments of true introspection and spiritual discovery.

These discipleships were essential for me to understand and experience the love of Jesus in a personal and practical way. Through the guidance and teachings received, I began to understand the concept of true repentance and the importance of living a life aligned with God's principles. This learning process has not only shaped my spiritual outlook but has also profoundly influenced my character and outlook on life.

Spending my adolescence at Iris was an invaluable experience, especially in a context where many young people in Mozambique face significant challenges and end up straying from the path. The structure and support I received were fundamental to my personal and spiritual development, and I am immensely grateful to have lived this phase in such an enriching and protective environment.

During this time, I learned valuable lessons about right and wrong, and the importance of making conscious choices. Furthermore, Iris Ministries emphasized the importance of education as a crucial means to overcome poverty and achieve success. The education I received was not just academic preparation, but a vital tool for my empowerment and personal fulfillment.

Knowing Jesus and having access to quality education were, without a doubt, essential tools for my success. These experiences gave me a solid foundation on which to build my future. Despite the challenges and difficulties I faced, the constant guidance from missionaries and educators was a crucial anchor on my journey. Not only have they helped me navigate life's ups and downs, but they have also taught me the value of discipline and time management.

I learned the importance of respecting schedules and being punctual, a lesson that was reflected in my academic and professional life. The ability to meet deadlines and maintain a commitment to punctuality has become a defining characteristic in my life, positively impacting my performance at college and at work.

In short, my adolescence at Iris Zimpeto was a phase of great learning and growth. The combination of a solid spiritual foundation and a quality education has provided me with the tools I need to face life's challenges and pursue my purpose with determination. I am deeply grateful for having had the opportunity to experience this phase in an environment that contributed so much to my personal and spiritual development.

My Journey of Dreams and Achievements

When I arrived at Iris Ministries, my life was marked by a lack of clear goals and defined dreams. From that moment, my journey became more about discovering my path and understanding what my true passions were. Over time, something began to form within me, a growing passion for football. This interest gave me a way to express myself and find joy, but I soon realised there was something deeper developing.

As I matured, my vision began to expand, and the idea of becoming a mechanical engineer began to gain traction. This new dream came from a combination of a fascination with how things work and a determination to create something meaningful. I then decided to dedicate myself hard to my studies, knowing that mechanical engineering would be the field where I could channel my passion for solving problems and developing innovative projects.

The path to achieving this dream was not easy, but the determination and support I received were fundamental. In 2022, I managed to achieve one of the biggest milestones of my life by graduating in mechanical engineering. My specialisation focused on producing engineering project drawings aimed at manufacturing aluminium windows. During my training, I acquired valuable skills in creating technical solutions and implementing projects that required precision and creativity.

After graduating, I started working as a designer, a role that allowed me to apply my knowledge and skills to real projects. My experience involved contributing to the design of doors, gates and windows for courts and large buildings in Mozambique. The opportunity to work on large-scale and impactful projects was extremely rewarding and challenging. Each project was not just a technical job, but a chance to leave a visible and lasting mark on the country's infrastructure.

Looking back, it's almost unbelievable to reflect on the journey I've taken from having no set goals to realizing those ambitious dreams. The feeling of having achieved these goals is a true miracle, highlighting the vital importance of the perseverance, passion and support I received along the way. Each challenge overcome, and each achievement, are testimonies that, with determination and faith, it is possible to transform dreams into reality and achieve goals that previously seemed unattainable.

My Spiritual Journey

My spiritual journey at Iris Global has been a trajectory of profound transformations and miracles, with the discovery of and relationship with Jesus standing out as the greatest blessing of my life. From the earliest years of my childhood, I felt a special connection with Jesus. Although at the time I didn't fully understand the depth of this relationship, there was a sincere affection and a longing to understand more about Him.

As I grew older and transitioned into adolescence, my involvement in dance groups and discipleship became a crucial aspect of my spiritual life. Participating in these groups was not only a way to express my faith creatively, but also an opportunity to delve deeper into the Word of God and Christian principles. These moments of dancing and teaching strengthened my faith, helping me see God's presence in every aspect of life and develop a more mature, personal understanding of His love and purpose.

In 2012, I took a significant step forward by becoming a Sunday School teacher. This experience was not only a great blessing for me, but also a privilege and a responsibility that I embraced dearly. As a teacher, my mission was to help children take their first steps into the Christian faith. Working with these young minds and hearts has given me a new perspective on the simplicity and beauty of the Gospel. Through teaching, I saw how faith can take root from an early age and how each little truth can become a solid foundation for a lifetime of spirituality and growth.

Each stage of this spiritual journey in Iris Global has been marked by moments of learning, growth and miracles that have reaffirmed my faith. Watching the transformation of children as they begin to understand and live the Christian faith, and witnessing how Jesus works in their lives from the beginning, have been an enriching and deeply rewarding experience. The walk with Jesus, from the earliest days of innocence to active involvement in His mission, has been the anchor of my life, giving me constant purpose and joy.

Special Thanks

Many people played a crucial role in my life while I was at Arco-Iris, and I would like to express my gratitude to each of them in a very special way:
- Papa Rolland and Mama Aida Baker - I want to sincerely thank this amazing couple for founding Iris Minis-

tries. Your vision and commitment to creating a space of love, acceptance and service, transformed not only my life, but the lives of many others. Your inspiring leadership and tireless dedication to God and others laid the foundation for a ministry that makes a real difference in the world.
- Papa Steve and Mana Ros - I am deeply grateful to you for welcoming me with so much affection and generosity at Iris Ministries in Zimpeto. The way you welcomed me and made me feel like part of the family had a profound impact on my life. Your love and support were fundamental to my personal and spiritual growth, providing me with a solid and secure foundation at crucial moments.
- Mana Katy Mueller (née Pleasance) and Mana Laura Kohl (née Anderson) - I am immensely grateful to you for giving me a spectacular and unforgettable childhood. The experiences, moments of joy and special care you gave me during this formative phase of my life created precious memories that I will cherish forever. The loving and nurturing environment you provided helped me grow and develop in a unique way.
- Mano Jonny and Mana Becky Wakeley - I am deeply grateful to you for the attentive care and guidance you gave me during my adolescence. You were a safe haven during a phase of many changes and challenges. Your continuous support, patience and genuine interest in my well-being were crucial to my development and overcoming the difficulties of that stage of life.
- Mana Sónia and Mana Clara - I want to express my sincere gratitude to you for your discipleship that had a profound impact during my adolescence. The teachings, spiritual guidance, and support you offered were

essential in deepening my relationship with Jesus and strengthening my faith. The wisdom and care with which you led discipleship helped me find a purpose and grow spiritually.
- Dominic, Petrus and Alta, Phil and Anna, and Rachel Clarke – you all were extraordinary missionaries who made a significant impact on my life during the time we spent together. The work you did and the example you set as missionary leaders not only enriched my experience at Iris Global, but also shaped my outlook on service and mission in the world.

Conclusion

My story is a testimony of strength and resilience, marked by a journey full of challenges and achievements. From my difficult childhood, where economic difficulties and family instability were constant, to the realisation of my dreams, each stage was a test of perseverance and faith. The adversity I faced from an early age shaped my character and taught me to value every small victory.

The unwavering support from the wonderful people I met at Iris Global in Zimpeto was crucial to my transformation. This shelter not only provided me with a safe home, but it also offered me opportunities for growth and education that seemed unattainable in the past. The guidance and care I received helped me overcome obstacles that, at first glance, seemed insurmountable.

I am deeply grateful to everyone who contributed to my journey, from the Iris Global staff and volunteers to the friends and mentors who believed in me. Every gesture of support, every word of encouragement, was fundamental to my personal development and success. This support network allowed me to turn challenges into opportunities and dreams into reality.

Now, with a heart full of gratitude, I hope to continue passing on the love and wisdom I have received. My goal is to use my experience and knowledge to inspire and help others who are facing similar adversity, just as I was helped. This commitment to giving back is how I intend to honour God's grace and support that has shaped my life.

Prayer

Lord God, I thank you for the light you placed in my life through Iris Ministries. You turned my pain into hope and my difficulty into triumph. I ask that you continue to guide me and use my life to do good, just as You did for me. May I be a reflection of Your love and an inspiration to others, just as I was inspired by those who came before me. In the name of Jesus, Amen.

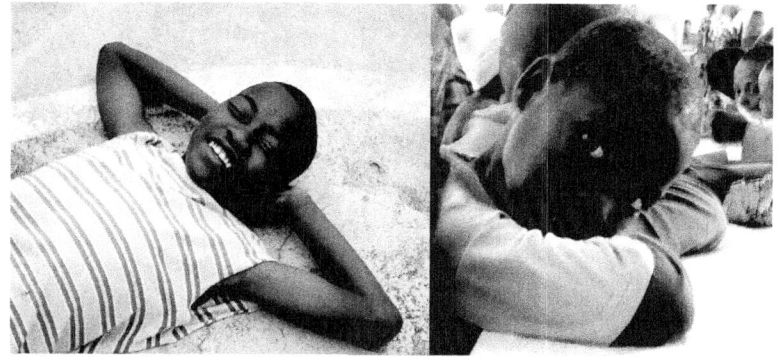

Silavio as a child on the base

University graduation　　　*At work*

Silavio at church with artwork for the book.

CHAPTER 21

Sina Armando

MY NAME IS Sina Armando, and I have lived and grown up my whole life on the Iris Global base in Zimpeto, Mozambique.

I do not remember much about my first months at Zimpeto as I was just a baby when I arrived. I was born on 22 August 2006, and arrived in Zimpeto five weeks later weighing just 1.6 kg. This first part of my story is simply what other people - the Mozambican tias (aunties) and the missionaries who cared for me - have told me.

My mother died shortly after I was born, and my father did not really know how to care for me: he was just giving me three bottles a day – breakfast, lunch and supper. Because I was not doing well, he took me to a government clinic in the city and was trying to give me away to one of the women in the waiting rooms. He wanted me to live. One of the doctors heard what was happening and they called Iris.

The next day, one of the tias from the centre came to collect me and took me back to the Iris Ministries baby house, home for about 32 babies and toddlers.

I was very sick and malnourished, and one of the missionaries wondered if I would even live through the first night. I did not sleep in the Baby House because I was so little. Mana Ros and one of the other missionaries, Mana Hilda, would feed me 20 ml of milk every hour as my tummy was so small. It meant they did not sleep very much, so other missionaries started to help, and every day I moved from one house to another in a wicker Moses basket, with all my clothes, diapers and bottles and the missionaries would care for me. I was still only drinking a tiny amount of milk every two hours, so I do not think anyone got much sleep!

I am told that Christians all over the world – from Australia to Canada, from England to America - were praying for me to live.

Little by little, I gained weight (I loved my milk!), grew stronger and healthier until it was safe enough for me to live in the Baby House with all the other children. There were six babies there, all about the same age as me and I am sure we kept everyone busy. Seventeen years later some of us are still friends and see each other frequently.

I lived in the Baby House for the first four years of my life and although I was small, I was very active, and some would say "feisty"! I was not always healthy though. In fact, there were many medical issues in my early years. I remember (from photos) having chicken pox and being covered in spots. Then I got malaria and ended up in hospital with one of the tias caring for me.

When I was four years old, late one afternoon I started having a convulsion. I had not been sick and did not have a fever, so it was all very strange. Two nurses rushed me to the big government hospital (thirty minutes away) – one was driving and speaking to the head of the Baby House, one was helping me breathe.

Again, very quickly, many people around the world were praying for me. When we arrived, the government paediatric emergency room was empty – unheard of – and quickly three doctors were working to treat me. I was admitted to the Intensive Care Unit and eventually made a full recovery. To this day, we never knew what caused the convulsion, but now, as a teenager, what I do know is that God protected and saved my life once again.

Jeremiah 29:11 talks about God's plans and purposes for our lives, plans that will bring good and not harm, plans for hope and a future. Again and again, I can testify to God protecting me from harm on so many occasions.

This is another example ....

When I was in 1st Grade, one of the other students gave me "medicine juice" to drink – and very quickly I started vomiting and not feeling good. One of the other small boys went to get help and (again) I was rushed to hospital where they treated me until I was feeling well again. Survivor is my middle name!

Until I was four, I lived in the Baby House but then, with five of my friends we moved to a small "transition" house with Mana Tracey (missionary). After a year (or sometimes two) children moved out of there into the bigger dormitories on the centre – but I stayed. An older girl, Felismina, already lived with Mana Tracey and, as the years have passed, she has become just like a sister to me.

We both still live with Mana Tracey in a house on the Iris Base. I like living with Mana Tracey and Felismina because, ever since I was little, she has looked after me, especially when I have been so sick. Felismina and I have even been to England to visit Mana Tracey's church and family.

Growing up on the centre we would always go to church, and I loved the singing and dancing. Every Easter we would show the Jesus film out on the soccer field so other people could come and hear about Jesus. When I was seven, I remember when they called people to come to the front and accept Jesus into their hearts. I told the missionary that I wanted to go. I will remember that night forever. Over the years, I have enjoyed Bible Camps and Retreats which have helped me to grow in my faith. In 2022, at the end of a big conference on our centre, both Felismina and I (and lots of other girls) were baptised early one morning in the Indian Ocean.

The biggest challenges of my life began when I was eight years old. For a very long time I kept losing my voice. I could hardly talk (it was as if I always had laryngitis) and I kept being sent to ER for breathing difficulties – everyone thought I had asthma. I can remember thinking I was going to die.

I felt very sad because the other children would tease me. They said I had a voice like an old man, and I did not like it! Finally, we went to see Dr Machava at one of the private clinics in Maputo and, after hearing me speak, he explained to the missionaries that he thought I had a chronic illness called "Recurrent Respiratory Papillomatosis", and that there were papillomas (small nodules) growing on my vocal cords, which were slowly blocking my airway.

Missionaries and their friends quickly asked people to pray and help with the costs of a private operation. A few weeks later, I had the operation, and the surgeon removed over forty papillomas. I had to stay in hospital for two nights and I remember Papa Steve bringing me balloons! I could only eat soup and jelly for three days. At night in the hospital, I was scared.

I had a second operation about ten weeks later, removing papillomas again and then Dr Machava said I could start having injections twice a week for three months as treatment.

We started going to the government hospital at 7 am twice a week to have the injections. I did NOT like it at all and the nurses and doctors (sometimes four of them) would have to hold me still. Those injections hurt a lot, and I always cried. Sometimes I was sick afterwards, and once I ended up having a convulsion – it was very scary.

Every few months I had to have a "scope" to check and see what was happening with the papillomas and the scars. Usually, I had to have an anaesthetic and go to the operating room, but one time they tried to do a scope without any anaesthetic. Four medical people held me down on a chair while the doctor put a tube down my throat. It was horrible and I cried for a long time afterwards.

After that, we went to South Africa for scopes and, in 2019, I had the last one – no more papillomas and no more scopes. I was still very self-conscious because my voice was very different, and people still teased me, so we started praying for my voice to be normal.

God has healed me, and slowly my voice has got better too. I am still quite self-conscious, but everyone tells me there is nothing wrong with my voice. I like to sing and can play the guitar a little and everyone says I like to talk a lot!

As I have learned to read my Bible, my favourite scripture has become Ecclesiastes 3 – "A time for Everything". The first time I was brave enough to speak in our Thursday night church service, I shared from this verse.

When I think about my life, there have been lots of very sad and difficult times – but lots of happy times, too. Most of the sad times are because of my health challenges, times in hospital and not knowing my family.

When my mum died, I was so little, and it was only my dad who would come and visit me very occasionally as I was growing up on the centre. He was an older man, but he would bring me cookies and always come and ask how I was doing at school.

School has not been easy. It took me a long time to learn to read and, with being so sick, I had to repeat a class as I missed so many lessons. While I was spending so much time in the hospital and missing school, Mana Tracey found a stables where I could have riding lessons. She says it was because she wanted me to do something that was fun and give me a break from all the hours in the hospital. I liked riding and am still having lessons now. I like to canter and even do show jumping and a little bit of cross country and dressage.

Before Covid, we would have Gymkhanas and other competitions, even riding in pairs and in costumes (once I was "Beauty" and my partner was "The Beast"). I have a collection of rosettes on my bedroom wall as reminders of all those days.

Sadly, my dad never came to see me ride and, in 2022 he died. He had not visited me for a long time, which was not unusual. But then early one morning a tia phoned to tell us he was dead. He had been sick in a hospital very close to the centre, but I did not know and never got to visit him. When they told me, I started crying a lot. I can remember thinking that now my dad was with my mom in heaven and that now I had no one to come and visit me. I also know I asked Mana Tracey if he had died of COVID.

Two days later Mana Tracey, Felismina and the tias came with me to the funeral. It was a very long way away in a place called Calanga. It took us nearly four hours to get there, and was out in the bush. At the end there was not even a road to follow. When we got there, they had to put my dad's coffin on a tractor to take it to the graveside. There were lots and lots of people there – and lots of them were staring at me. Some of them did not know I was still alive. Some of them wanted to talk to me about my mum; others just wondered who I was.

At the funeral, I met some of my family for the first time. I knew that I had two half-brothers and a half-sister, but did not know all their children – my nephews and nieces. There were aunts and uncles (I think) there too. It was all very strange.

When they buried my dad, they put all his clothes and belongings in the grave too. There was a small hat and a wallet that I had bought him in England one time – and that made me cry.

We stayed in Calanga all day as there was a big feast. Some food I did not know. But I talked with my nephews and nieces, who are mostly the same age as me. My youngest nephew is four and I liked playing with him – and he liked playing with me. Some of us swapped our cell phone numbers – and now I knew I had some family.

When it was time to leave, I climbed on the tractor trailer with my family and had a ride out to the road with them before we said goodbye. They have not really kept in contact much and still no one has come to visit me on the centre but just last week (the anniversary of my dad's death) we planned for me to go and stay in my stepsister's house for two days.

I was very nervous and even thought I should pack a cup, spoon and plate (like going camping). Mana Tracey had always wanted me to know my family, so maybe this was the beginning. I had a good time, but the food was very different, and they had no electricity a lot of the time. I also missed my home on the centre even though I was only away for two nights.

I still have at least two more years of school to finish and, whilst I am studying, I am also making lots of cakes. Last year, four students from ninth grade (including me) were able to take a seven-week culinary course where we learned to make cakes, quiches and biscuits. I had been practicing a little bit at home and then Papa Steve and some visitors started asking me to make cakes for them. I have now made over 25 cakes and am saving money for a camera. I have a small business and must work out the cost of all the ingredients.

I am also getting braver, bolder, and more courageous about speaking in front of other people and, in June 2023, preached in front of all the secondary school students (about 600) in our school. I spoke about "Miracles", as God has been reminding me of how many miracles He has done in my life. I told everyone about the miracle God had done in healing my voice. A miracle brings about transformation, and I asked the school kids what did they want to be changed in their lives? What miracle did they want? No miracle is impossible for God: He can change anything.

I think my personal miracles are that I survived being so sick and malnourished as a baby, that God has healed me from the papillomas, and I have a voice that sounds normal. If you met me now, you would never know what had happened to me as a child.

I want to finish school and then go on to higher education. I have been fortunate enough to visit Kruger National Park on many occasions (on the way to doctors' consults) and I think I would like to work there either as a tour guide or in the restaurants. If I am good enough, I might like to have a cake-making business, and then I sometimes think I would like to be a lawyer because I like to speak up for what is right.

Another of my favourite bible verses is Romans 10:13, where it says, "Everyone who calls on the name of the Lord will be saved" – and that is my testimony.

In the beginning, other people called on the name of the Lord to save my life - when I was a tiny sick baby, and when I suffered convulsions. As I get older, I am learning to call on God's name for myself and ask for His continued protection. I still get allergic reactions, hives and other medical issues but, repeatedly, He has been good to me and kept me healthy and whole. As I look to my future, I know He will be in control, watching out for me and providing the very best.

Stories of Hope | 235

Sina loves horse riding

Sina turns 18. She has a cake business

Sina with friends Luís and Louísa

Sina with her "family" on the base - Mana Tracey's house

CHAPTER 22

Lourenço and Miguel Carimo

WE WERE BORN on the 27 February 2002, in a humble neighbourhood of Maputo city. From the beginning, our lives were marked by immense challenges. Despite much adversity, our dreams were big. We both wanted to be professional football players. This is the story of how we faced and overcame difficulties, found support, and demonstrated faith and resilience.

We grew up in a humble family, with our mother, Florinda, known as Dona Linda. When we were born, Dona Linda faced enormous difficulties. Unable to breastfeed, she was forced to beg on the streets of Maputo, to feed us and guarantee the basics for our family's survival.

In a moment of desperation and despair, she heard about Iris Global, an organisation that offered help to families in difficulty. She sought help and received milk, clothes and a little money to buy food. This support was crucial for our family's survival and helped alleviate some of our difficulties.

Unfortunately, our lives continued to be marked by problems. Our parents fought frequently and eventually separated. We were sent to live with our grandmother, hoping to find a more stable and safer environment.

Life with our grandmother seemed promising initially, but we soon discovered that she, too, was facing financial difficulties. Although she was a kind person, life with her did not lead to a better situation for us. Furthermore, the wider family took advantage of us, making us do heavy labour, and providing inadequate food.

The situation worsened when our mother became seriously ill. This increased the emotional and financial burden on us. We were forced to return home and live with our father, hoping the situation would improve. However, he also faced problems, and life remained difficult.

One night, our father was seized by severe pain. We tried to help him, but in vain. He passed away that night, leaving us in a state of shock and deep sadness. The loss of our father was a devastating blow for both of us.

After our father's death, we had to leave school to work and help support the household. We were exploited and used by people who took advantage of our plight. Our childhood was sacrificed in the name of survival.

In the midst of our difficulties, we found comfort in faith. We were invited to attend a church, and we came to know Jesus as Lord and Saviour. Our struggles began to seem more bearable. We believed that God was with us, and this gave us strength to face challenges.

With renewed faith, we decided to return to Iris Global for help. We met Augusto Lopes, the organisation's operations manager. Augusto heard our story and understood the difficulties we were facing. He explained that many people asked for help without really needing it, but he was willing to help us.

Iris Global provided us with essential support. We were helped to return to school and given a small job to help with clothing and food. With this support, our mother was also able to return home, which brought relief and hope to the family.

With the support of Iris Global, our home was improved. Although there was still much to do, our living conditions also began to improve. It was a small step toward a better life, and we felt like we were a little closer to our dreams becoming a reality.

We finished high school with good results. Despite the challenges described above, we dedicated ourselves to our studies and overcame many difficulties. We never lost faith that our future was in God's hands.

We dreamed of going to university to study International Relations. However, finances were an obstacle. Iris Global explained that there were not enough resources to cover University fees at that time. They offered support so we could continue our studies. Our dreams of university seemed distant, but we never lost faith.

Despite our financial difficulties, we were encouraged to undertake training in Physical Education. With a lot of effort and dedication, we completed the course and became Physical Education teachers. This was a big step for our careers and a breakthrough towards our dreams.

In addition to graduating as teachers, we also became professional football referees. We worked with the Mozambique national team and used our skills and experiences to contribute to the sport we have always loved.

Despite these achievements, our dream of taking a Higher Education course in International Relations is still alive. We continue working to achieve this goal. We believe that with faith and effort, anything is possible.

Influenced by our own experiences and the help we had received, we aspired to make a difference in the lives of children with motor and physical disabilities. The idea of assisting these children, with physical exercises and massage, has always been present in our hearts.

We asked Iris Global for the resources needed to start an assistance programme for special needs children. Knowing our commitment and seriousness, the ministry decided to support this new venture.

We have been working for three years helping children with special needs at Iris Global in Zimpeto. We apply our acquired knowledge in physical exercises and massage. We have seen significant improvements in the children's motor coordination and balance. Our work not only contributes to their development, but also serves as a source of inspiration for those around us.

In addition to working with the special needs children, we have become Physical Education teachers. We use our experiences and skills to teach and motivate students in the school on the base. We promote the importance of physical activity and health.

We continue to work on our dreams. We still feel the desire to expand our programmes to reach more children and get new qualifications to improve our skills even more. The quest for knowledge and skill enhancement is an essential part of our journey.

We reflect on our trajectory and realise how far we have come from the hard times of our childhood.

Iris Global played a crucial role in our lives. The organisation's support was essential for us to overcome difficulties and achieve our goals. We are grateful for the help that we have received, and we continue to be living proof of the positive impact that community support can have.

Today, we use our stories of overcoming to encourage others. Our childhood was marked by difficulties, but our trajectory is a reminder that even in the worst circumstances, faith, dedication and the right support can transform lives and make a lasting impact on the community. With determination and support it is possible to overcome any obstacle and achieve the most audacious dreams.

Miguel as a youth   *Lourenço as a youth*

International soccer referee

Interview on TV

Graduation from University - with Mum

In church - off to America next week

CHAPTER 23

Ana Samu

M*y name is* Ana Malunguissa Samu. I was born in 1953 and I am seventy-one years old. I am the mother of five children. I was born in Zimbabwe.

My mother died when I was 12 years old, and my father died when I was 15. I was not able to go to school because I didn't have any money. However, my aunty and uncle cared for me. He was a farmer of cows but there was not much money in the house.

I helped my uncle for three years with the cows. After these years he gave me a calf which I cared for until it was old enough to sell. With this money I bought a small house, and I kept working as a farmer of cows. I lived for a small amount of time in this house on my own.

I was 18 years old when I married my first husband. I had 2 children with this man. My first husband beat me a lot, so my family told me to separate from him.

I continued to live on my own in my small house. I then met a man who was a soldier in the Frelimo Mozambican army.

In 1980 we moved to live in Mozambique. We lived close to the border of Zimbabwe but in Mozambique.

At this time Mozambique was in a civil war which lasted for 16 years. We often had to leave our house to hide in the bush because Renamo (the opposition army) was fighting close to the border and were killing the Frelimo soldiers. We were very poor, living in the bush moving a lot so he would not be found by Renamo. We slept under the trees and did not eat or drink sometimes for three or more days. We were so thirsty we could not swallow, and our mouths were so dry we had to drink our own urine.

Sometimes we ate the grass and weeds so we could have something in our stomachs. One of my close friends who was with her husband, (who was also a soldier), died during this time because of hunger and thirst. This time was very hard for me. Some of the women ran away from their husbands, but I stayed with mine.

My children were born in the bush, where there was no specialised medical help for the birthing process. Thanks be to God; all of my children were born healthy.

Much later my husband was transferred to various provinces including Tete, Niassa and Nampula. I had three of my four children in these provinces. Only my last son was born in Maputo.

I remember when we moved from Tete to Nampula-Lichinga. On that journey, there was an attack from armed bandits and many people lost their lives. However, thanks be to God our lives were spared. We arrived in Nampula safely.

In 1998 we finally left Nampula for Maputo, to the suburb of Maguanine where my last child was born. My husband then left the military to work with the government in immigration. I finally thought everything was going to be fine with our family.

I stayed with this husband until 2012 when he left me to

marry another woman. This was very difficult because I had remained with him for a long time during the war - a time of great difficulty - and I thought we would have a good life.

It had started in 2001, when my husband began to leave the house for long periods of time, leaving me alone with all of the children. This was a very hard time, as we were very hungry with all kinds of difficulties. It was at this time that I started doing jobs in community houses in exchange for food or even some clothes or funds to support my children.

In 2004, I went to the home of Mana Ana Jamu. There I found that eight children from the Iris Ministries centre in Zimpeto were living with her. These children were under the umbrella of Iris Ministries and had previously been living in the house of Papa Steve and Mana Rosa. These eight children were not the biological children of Papa Steve and Mana Rosa.

After years of caring for them in their own home, Papa Steve and Mana Rosa had wanted the children to experience normal Mozambican life in the community. I could see that the children were loved and cared for.

It was at this time that Ana Jamu gave me some work; helping her in the community house. We lived there for three years and then, in 2007, the eight children, Ana and I moved back to the Iris centre in Zimpeto.

When we arrived at the center, Mana Ros welcomed me and said for me to feel at home. When I started this work, I found peace. I want to thank Papa Steve and Mana Rosa for that first day when Mana Rosa said, "Welcome to our house, work in peace with us." Those words lifted my spirit and gave me the courage and force to work with all my heart.

I was so happy there because I had a really good job loving the children. In the following days Mana Rosa said to me to be full of joy for what God has given me. Those words deeply moved my heart. Since that day I assumed that in my work

I was serving a mission that God had trusted to me. I love the work God has given me.

When I started working with the eight children, they were between seven and eight years old. Now, in 2024, they are all adults and are no longer living on the Iris Zimpeto base. Thanks be to God that all these children both love and respect me, and I have good relations with them now that they have grown. God gave me this work and I have worked without problem and fighting in this job.

From 2019, when the last child left the house of Papa Steve and Mana Rosa I was given work in the preschool, the girls' area, and more recently in the older girls' dormitory.

In 2023, at the age of seventy, I was due for my retirement from work. Through the generosity of Papa Steve and Mana Rosa, I have continued to help the older girls in their transition house. I will formally retire at the end of 2024.

I thank God for the life of Papa Steve and Mana Rosa as they allowed me to have the opportunity to work with the children and to love them all into their futures. Their love and affection for me helped in my understanding of life. I go to church every day and thank God for his faithfulness to me all through my life.

I will be retiring soon. I hope to do a small business with a small shop to sell things or to raise chickens to make money.

Thank you so much to my God.

Stories of Hope | 249

Ana Samu with Ana Etel, Lija (one of the eight children) and Mana Ros

Ana with girls from "top house"

Mana Ros, Ana Samu, Papa Steve and Ana Etel

CHAPTER 24

Nilza Vincent

My name is Nilza Sequina Vincent. I am 38 years old and was born in 1986. I was born in Maputo province, Mozambique.

When my mother gave birth to me she was underage: she was only 12 years old. My father did not accept the pregnancy and my mother had to bear the burden of pregnancy alone.

My mother had a disturbed way of life during her pregnancy. She drank a lot and did not stay home. When I was born she did not stay with me. She left me with other family members before I was one year old but they did not have time to take care of me.

My family said that my mother had no time to care for her daughter; she only had time to drink. For this reason, no one wanted to know me.

One day, the sister of my grandmother saw the difficult situation I was going through and she took me to live with her. When I was just seven years old, she passed away. This was very sad for me because she had been like a mother to me. For this reason, I had to go back to where I lived before.

Going back there was terrifying for me. When I arrived, my mother went away to South Africa to search for better living conditions. I was left with my mother's family: two uncles, an aunt and her daughter. My aunt mistreated me as she was jealous that my mother was in South Africa "eating well" yet could not care for her biological daughter. During this time, my aunt would beat me. People saw what my aunt did with me and went to tell my mother that her daughter was suffering.

My mother sent someone to bring me to South Africa illegally. When I got to South Africa, I discovered that my mother had a new baby: I had a sister.

My sister's father did not live with my mother. My mother did not have any work, and lived from prostitution. Whenever my mother went out to work, I looked after my new sister. When my mother came home she said I was not taking good care of my sister, and she beat me. This continued every day. The saddest thing was that she would beat me, and the next day would not remember doing this.

A day came when my mother told me to steal money from a neighbour. I said to her that I could not steal. She said, "If you refuse to steal the money, then I will send you away from the house." So, in great fear I went to the neighbour's house and stole the money, so that my mother would not send me away. The neighbour realized that she no longer had money in her house and she knew my mother had sent me to steal. As a result, we were evicted from the house my mother was renting.

I was so tired of all the dramas and trauma I lived through with my mother, that I asked her to send me back to Mozambique. She accepted this proposal, and sent someone to go back with me to Mozambique. By the time I arrived at my family's house, I was 10 years old.

My other aunt, who is my mother's sister, asked me to live with her in Machava and help care for her son. However, I did not stay long with her because she did not want to enrol me in school, so I could not study.

I went back to the family house again. My aunt - who mistreated me - was no longer living there because she did not treat her brother well. So, in that house, it was just my two uncles and me. I went on to take care of the house. I was cooking and washing my uncles' clothes. At this time, I was 12 years of age. It was very difficult to leave the house. Whenever I tried to leave, my uncle would beat me. I was really tired of being beaten in every place I lived.

I decided to look for my father's house. It was not so far away. Upon finding my father's house, I encountered his brother, my uncle. He welcomed me into the house and had many questions for me. I said I wanted to talk to my father. He replied that my father had died. I asked my uncle if I could live with him in my father's house. He said this was OK and I did not need go back to the other house any more.

At this time, I was 13 years old. I was not able to go to school because there was no money. To support myself, I made chamussas (pastries) to sell. This helped with all the household expenses.

My time in this house with my uncle was the worst of all the houses I lived in. All the problems that happened in this house fell on my shoulders. Living with my father's brother was one of the worst experiences. I lost all hope there, and I could not return to the other family house.

However, in 1999 another relative, who worked as a teacher at Iris Ministries, heard about my situation. He spoke to my uncle about me studying at the Iris Ministries school. My uncle accepted the proposal. I started studying there at 14 years of age. Things were not going well at home, and so I asked the director of Iris Ministries if I could live at the base. Living at the Zimpeto base was the best thing that happened in my life. I would keep to myself and just smile at everyone. I was determined not to get into trouble and not have friends. I kept myself to myself and did not provoke anyone or allow others to provoke me.

Time passed by and I got to know a missionary called Mana Corrie. Mana Corrie and Mana Rika opened the baby house in 2000 as there was no baby house before then: all the babies had been living in the girls' area. Mana Corrie invited me to help with the babies. This was a great joy to me because I really loved playing with babies and caring for them. I was now 15 years of age. The babies became my friends and gave me so much joy.

Many things changed in my life for the better. I received Jesus as my Lord and Saviour. While working in the baby house, I met a visitor from America named Barbara. We got on so well. She invited me to come to Hawaii for a visit.

In 2005, I travelled to Hawaii, and while there I received notification that my mother had lost her life. She had been very sick before dying. I was now an orphan, without mother or father. This made no difference to me as neither of them had true love for me.

It was very good to be in Hawaii for a month. I was now 17 years old.

After I came back from Hawaii, I continued to study and completed tenth grade. Then, at 21 years of age I stopped studying.

In 2009, I got married to my husband, Florindo. Then, in 2011, I began helping with consults in the Iris Ministries' clinic. I made appointments for the HIV positive children and accompanied them to their consults in the city. I have continued to do this work ever since. I love working with the children.

In addition to that work, I have a catering business. I make cakes and prepare meals for parties. I have completed several culinary courses.

In 2015, I was baptised and, since then, have been a helper in the local church in Khongolote. I coordinate the Sunday School classes.

Florindo and I now live in a neighbourhood near the Zimpeto base. We have three children. All of them are boys and are very beautiful people. Florindo and I love them very much.

My life has not been easy, but I am grateful to God because of what His Word says in John 16:33: "I have told you these things so that in me you may have peace. In this world you will have trouble. But take heart! I have overcome the world."

Thank you for the opportunity to share my testimony. I pray that God's grace is with all of you reading this story.

Nilza as a child   *Nilza and Florindo's wedding day*

Family photos

CHAPTER 25

Felismina Almeida

I ARRIVED AT Arco Iris Zimpeto when I was four years old, in July of 2004. I was bought to the centre by a family member (an Aunt I think) who was sleeping rough on the streets underneath a bench where she sold fruits and vegetables.

I only weighed eight kg. I didn't know how to walk and I couldn't talk. Nobody thought that I would learn to walk or speak because I was so weak and small.

I lived in the Baby House with over 30 other young children. One girl, Carmina, became my friend and protector. Even today, 20 years later, she is still one of my very best friends.

I remember that, when I was little, I had problems with my vision and would go to hospital for consults in the ambulance. Without really knowing what happened, my eyes got better and now, as an adult my vision is fine.

I didn't start going to school until I was 8 years old, and even then, I only went part of the time because I was still very weak and small. I remember learning to write on a chalkboard in the garden and slowly starting to learn. At the end of my first grade year, I won a prize for being the best student in class.

I am still very small. Even now, aged 24, I wear clothing for 11 to 12-year-olds, and the effects of malnutrition mean that my body has not grown. I have weak bones and a curved spine, and I find walking a long distance hard – but that doesn't matter.

My favourite verse in the Bible is Mark 10: 27: "All things are possible with God." I can see that there are many things in my life that have happened because God made it possible.

When I started school, we thought I would study until fifth grade and learn to read and write a little. When I got to fifth grade I passed and then we decided I would study until the national exams in seventh grade. I passed those exams, and although some people thought I should finish school, I wanted to keep going! My favourite subjects were Portuguese, English and Biology.

During those years, I joined our sewing program on the centre. Once again, many people thought learning to sew would be too difficult for me, but a missionary called Mana Betty helped and encouraged me. She taught me how to use a sewing machine and always let me do the same sewing projects as the other girls. Now I have my own sewing machine at home. I still join the sewing program when I am on holidays.

I carried on studying, but then Covid shut all the schools in Mozambique. I had failed some of my tenth grade subjects before Covid which meant I had to resit the exams a year later. Then, with Covid closures it was another year (three years in total) before I passed tenth grade. Once again, everyone thought I should stop but I wanted to continue to study until twelfth grade.

In November 2023, aged 23, I finished my secondary school education. I had taken the same exams as everyone else and passed! My school had a big "Prom" night where all the girls wore purple/lilac dresses. Purple is my favourite colour. We danced, sang and ate, and were awarded our final certificates.

I also won a prize for my persistence and positive attitude throughout my school years. My cheerful outlook – despite my physical and health challenges – meant that I was often chosen to represent the school when we had visitors. One of my special memories was being presented to the First Lady of Mozambique, Isaura Nyusi, when she visited the school.

My early years of malnourishment have permanently affected my bones and I live with scoliosis and osteoporosis. Twice a year, I visit a doctor in South Africa so we can measure any changes to my body.

Through all these years, I have lived with one of the long-term Iris Missionaries, Mana Tracey. She began caring for me when I was little (I arrived on the centre when she was visiting from England) and I have lived with her and two other girls ever since.

When I was seven, she was able to get a passport for me, and I started visiting South Africa.

In 2015, I went to England with her and my "sister" (Sina). I had never been on a plane, but I was very excited – and loved the journey. My best memories of that time were visiting London, seeing Windsor Castle, riding on buses that said, "Next Stop!" and meeting many, many people who had been praying for me and Iris Zimpeto. I hope I can visit again one day.

Psalm 23 is another one of my favourite passages in the Bible, because it says I will lack nothing. I know God has been very faithful in protecting my life and providing for me. My physical health limitations are always a challenge. I fall frequently and have had several trips to A & E and some stitches - but so far haven't broken any bones.

When I am out in the city, I know people stop and look at me, especially in the shopping malls. I look very different to other 24-year-olds but, I love fashionable clothes and make-up.

When I finished school, I had to decide what to do next.

One idea was to help somewhere on the Iris Zimpeto base – but I wanted to study! I really wanted to be a nurse and care for other people. I talked to lots of people, and everyone said that nursing would be too difficult or me. I was a little bit sad as it was my dream.

Mana Tracey and Mano Dalberto helped me look for other options, and, finally, we found a course in Nutritional Science. The one problem was that the course was downtown and it would be difficult to get there. Yet, as the Bible says, "I can do all things through Christ" – and now I am a 1st year student, studying a course that means I can care for other people – and travelling to the centre of Maputo every day. I wake up at 4am to catch a school bus at 4:50 and I have breakfast when I get to the Institute. My classes are from 7:30am – 12:20pm every morning, and then I ride public transport home. Some of the bus drivers know me now and even save me a seat. Sometimes I don't even have to pay!

I study Biochemistry, Anthropology, Anatomy, Public Health, Biology and English (for Health Services) and my favourite module is Biochemistry.

When I arrived at Iris Zimpeto as a very sick, malnourished child, no one but God could have imagined what my life would look like 20 years later. I don't think anyone imagined I would still be alive! God has had a good plan for me forever. I learnt about Him a lot growing up on the centre and, in 2022, I was baptised as a sign of my commitment to Him.

One of my favourite worship songs, which we sing frequently in our church, is called "Yesu Wakanaka". It means – "Jesus is VERY Good".

I know! He has been very good to me.

Stories of Hope | 261

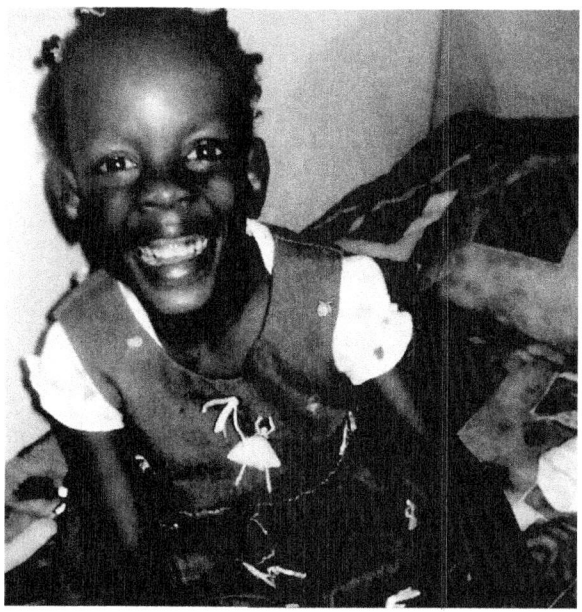

Felismina as a child

School days

At home with Mana Tracey and girls

School graduation

CHAPTER 26

It's all about Jesus

I DEBATED LONG and hard how to end this book.
Suggestions were made to perhaps write a brief history of Mozambique – or maybe just finish with a simple scripture – or some more testimonies. But I wish to finish with sharing about the miraculous.

Iris is built on five core values, one of which is dependence on the miraculous: the power of Jesus.

> "Very truly, I tell you, whoever believes in me will do the works I have been doing, and they will do even greater things than these, because I am going to the Father. And I will do whatever you ask in my name, so that the Father may be glorified in the Son. You may ask me for anything in my name and I will do it." (John 14: 12-14)

> "Jesus has a lot of power. Jesus is not just a wonderful guy, and he is not just a good example. When we're facing tough stuff, we need someone who's more than just

an example. We need the Lord. He's got life and POWER. If I love Jesus totally, then I value his power. We want everything in Iris to be miraculous. That includes money, food, life, breath, etc. The way Iris functions and how far we have gotten is because we look to Jesus always. Whether it is a blind person seeing, a malnourished child fed, an abandoned baby loved into life or millions of dollars required, miracles are needed every day." (Rolland Baker)

We see many miracles in Mozambique, because the people know they really need a miracle. The 25 testimonies in this book are all miraculous encounters with a real God who cares.

As you know, Jesus' first miracle is the wedding at Cana, where he turns water into wine (John 2: 1-11). The question I ask is, "Why did Jesus do this?" Why did he turn the water into wine? Why didn't he raise a dead person, or at least find a lame man at the wedding and see him walk? With all the big problems happening, who really cares about there not being enough wine at a wedding? We live in a world where there a lot of people, and many *big* problems: war, hunger, floods, sickness, unemployment and more. Why should God be interested in our *little* problems, like whether there's enough wine at a wedding?

Turning the water into wine was a simple and practical kind of miracle, but it shows Jesus' concern for those normal, practical and small problems in our lives.

Are our problems too small for him? It is true that there are always people worse off than us. We might have the flu but someone else has cancer. We might think our house is too small, but thousands lost their houses during the floods of Mozambique when we first arrived in 2000. We can't find a job, but there are others who have nothing, and who are really, hungry. Yet that is why Jesus turned the water into wine. If something is important to us, it is important to Jesus. This is so for the poorest of the poor in Mozambique, and for those of us who live in a comfortable Western setting. Jesus really cares about the ordinary things in our lives.

Let us look at a big miracle. I love the story of Lazarus: a great story of the miraculous (John 11: 38-44). There are two distinctive parts to this story. Both demand all our attention.

First, Lazarus was dead. He'd been there for four days – he was DEAD!! So, what Jesus did was big. A real, 100%, all in all, top of the tree miracle. If Jesus did this, He wants us to do the same: to pray for the sick, let blind eyes see, the lame walk, cancer to be healed and the dead to be raised. We pray, but it is *Jesus* who does the miracle. When we realise it is Jesus who does the miracle, it takes the pressure off us. Sometimes we spend so much time looking at what *we* do: the atmosphere, the music, the setting, how we pray, what we pray, the condition of this or that – when it is about HIM. *He* does the miracle. The miraculous occurs when we find his presence.

Second, there is something we can do as well as praying. Jesus said to those around the tomb, "Take off the grave clothes and set him free" (v 44). You see, Jesus does the miracle, and we undo the grave clothes. It is not one or the other, it is *both*: calling on Jesus to do the miraculous *and* taking off grave clothes. In Mozambique we spend most of our time undoing grave clothes. For example, we build houses, and provide community clinics, a community school, a baby milk programme and a food box programme (giving a box of basic food supplies to 40 families weekly).

So, I encourage you to pray for others, whether for a sore toe, terminal cancer, a headache, a person without a job, a lonely person, a hungry family or a blind person. It is all important to Jesus. He wants to do the miracles. And for the miracle that you need, *do* something. Don't just sit and wait. The people unwrapped Lazarus' bandages. Like those around Lazarus, be there to unwrap bandages. Do not make small of what God does: water into wine, a headache gone, feeling happier, the dead raised: all are miraculous.

STEVEN LAZAR is a missionary with Iris Global in Mozambique. Steven and his wife Rosalind have voluntarily served in the Children's centre in Maputo since 2001. Steven and Rosalind have a passion for children and to see them grow in their love for Jesus and give them opportunity to be educated, have good health and nutrition, and a future. When not in Mozambique, Steven and Rosalind love traveling and spending time with their family in Australia and Canada.

Printed in Great Britain
by Amazon